The War on Terrorism

COMBATING THE GLOBAL TERRORIST THREAT

The War on Terrorism

COMBATING THE GLOBAL TERRORIST THREAT

Titles in the American War Library series include:

The War on Terrorism
Leaders and Generals
Life of an American Soldier in Afghanistan
The War at Home
The War in Afghanistan
Weapons of War

The American Revolution

The Civil War

The Cold War

The Korean War

The Persian Gulf War

The Vietnam War

World War I

World War II

The War on Terrorism

COMBATING THE GLOBAL TERRORIST THREAT

by Thomas Streissguth

San Diego • Detroit • New York • San Francisco • Cleveland • New Haven, Conn. • Waterville, Maine • London • Munich

For more information, contact
Lucent Books
27500 Drake Rd.
Farmington Hills, MI 48331-3535
Or you can visit our Internet site at http://www.gale.com

LIBRARY OF CONGRESS CATALOGING-IN-PUBLICATION DATA

Streissguth, Thomas, 1958–
Combating the global terrorist threat / by Thomas Streissguth.
v. cm. — (American war library; the war on terrorism series)
Includes bibliographical references and index.
Contents: Counterterrorism abroad—Targeting sponsor states—Afghanistan—Iraq—the Philippines—Pakistan—Saudi Arabia—Europe and Great Britain.
ISBN 1-59018-327-4 (hardback : alk. paper)
1. Terrorism—Prevention—Juvenile literature. 2. War on Terrorism, 2001– —Juvenile literature. [1. Terrorism—Prevention. 2. War on Terrorism, 2001–] I. Title. II. American war library. War on terrorism series.
HV6431.S748 2004
973.931—dc22

2003014492

Printed in the United States of America

☆ Contents ☆

☆ Foreword ☆

A Nation Forged by War

The United States, like many nations, was forged and defined by war. Despite Benjamin Franklin's opinion that "There never was a good war or a bad peace," the United States owes its very existence to the War of Independence, one to which Franklin wholeheartedly subscribed. The country forged by war in 1776 was tempered and made stronger by the Civil War in the 1860s.

The Texas Revolution, the Mexican-American War, and the Spanish-American War expanded the country's borders and gave it overseas possessions. These wars made the United States a world power, but this status came with a price, as the nation became a key but reluctant player in both World War I and World War II.

Each successive war further defined the country's role on the world stage. Following World War II, U.S. foreign policy redefined itself to focus on the role of defender, not only of the freedom of its own citizens, but also of the freedom of people everywhere. During the Cold War that followed World War II until the collapse of the Soviet Union, defending the world meant fighting communism. This goal, manifested in the Korean and Vietnam conflicts, proved elusive, and soured the American public on its achievability. As the United States emerges as the world's sole superpower, American foreign policy has been guided less by national interest and more by protecting international human rights. But as involvement in Somalia and Kosovo proves, this goal has been equally elusive.

As a result, the country's view of itself changed. Bolstered by victories in World Wars I and II, Americans first relished the role of protector. But, as war followed war in a seemingly endless procession, Americans began to doubt their leaders, their motives, and themselves. The Vietnam War especially caused people to question the validity of sending its young people to die in places where they were not particularly wanted and for people who did not seem especially grateful.

While the most obvious changes brought about by America's wars have been geopolitical in nature, many other aspects of society have been touched. War often does not bring about change directly, but acts instead like the catalyst in a chemical reaction, accelerating changes already in progress.

Some of these changes have been societal. The role of women in the United States had been slowly changing, but World War II put thousands into the work force and into uniform. They might have gone back to being housewives after the war, but equality, once experienced, would not be forgotten.

Likewise, wars have accelerated technological change. The necessity for faster airplanes and more destructive bombs led to the development of jet planes and nuclear energy. Artificial fibers developed for parachutes in the 1940s were used in clothing of the 1950s.

Lucent Books' American War Library covers key wars in the development of the nation. Each war is covered in several volumes to allow for more detail, context, and to provide volumes on often neglected subjects, such as the kamikazes of World War II or the weapons used in the Civil War. As with all Lucent books, notes, annotated bibliographies, and appendixes such as glossaries give students a launching point for further research. In addition, sidebars and archival photographs enhance the text. Together, each volume in the American War Library will aid students in understanding how America's wars have shaped and changed its politics, economics, and society.

★ Introduction ★

A New Kind of War

On September 11, 2001, nineteen hijackers took command of four passenger airplanes and crashed them into targets in the eastern United States. Within hours of the attacks, government investigators concluded that a terrorist group known as al-Qaeda (meaning "the base" in Arabic), led by Osama bin Laden, was responsible for them. The U.S. government had been aware of al-Qaeda since the mid-1990s. The organization was suspected of carrying out attacks on two U.S. embassies, in Kenya and Tanzania, in 1998. Al-Qaeda operatives had also bombed the U.S. destroyer *Cole* in the port of Aden, the capital of the Middle Eastern nation of Yemen.

But although the government was aware of al-Qaeda, this knowledge did not prevent the September 11 attacks. Nor did it prepare the United States for the War on Terrorism. The U.S. military had not planned for direct attacks on civilian targets in the United States. Security at airports and at the nation's borders was lax. The borders were open, and thousands of foreigners were entering the country unmonitored every day; many of the September 11 hijackers had been living in the United States legally for several years.

Prior to September 11, most Americans could not imagine such a large-scale disaster. Although Americans had witnessed a few terrorist acts on their soil, most believed that terrorist violence happened in foreign countries. The bitter conflicts of the Middle East, Africa, and South Asia were distant events that many simply ignored. The United States had friendly neighbors on its borders, and two vast oceans separating it from distant trouble spots.

According to Michael A. Ledeen, in his book *The War Against the Terror Masters: Why It Happened. Where We Are Now. How We'll Win*, "Like few before us, we have only a very limited interest in the world outside our shores. We tend to our own affairs, and we have done it so successfully that we are the first

The south tower of New York's World Trade Center collapses in a cloud of dust and debris during the September 11, 2001, terrorist attacks.

people in history to believe peace is the normal condition of mankind."[1]

New Weapons and New Strategies

The attacks of September 11 brought the United States into a new kind of war. There are no front lines, as understood by military leaders, in the War on Terrorism. The enemy is not easily distinguishable from civilians. The al-Qaeda terrorists plot in secret "sleeper" cells, which remain quiet and inactive until called on to commit an attack. They move about freely, hold jobs, attend schools, and slip through airport security systems.

These new approaches mean the United States must defend itself in a new way. The massed infantry and armor of previous wars are useless against terrorists disguised as ordinary citizens and living regular lives. The enemy is not an army or military entity, but individuals and small groups, hiding in remote areas and among noncombatants in crowded cities. To win this war, undercover and police operations are more valuable than tanks, troops, and bombs.

While the United States searches for individual terrorists and terrorist groups, it also must deal with countries that sponsor or protect terrorists with shelter, arms, or money. American diplomats must work with these nations. They also have to strike deals, seek agreements, and form alliances with friendly countries whose military or police agencies can provide help. These alliances will change over time as nations follow their own interests and work to maintain their own security. For the United States, an individual nation might be an ally today, an enemy tomorrow, and a neutral party next week.

Above all, there will not be a declared victory in the War on Terrorism, nor a peace treaty ending hostilities. There will be periods of conventional military action, times of intense undercover operations to capture or kill enemy combatants, times of diplomatic wrangling, and times in which very little seems to happen. The War on Terrorism will appear and then disappear from television newscasts and newspaper headlines as citizens in the United States and elsewhere get on with their ordinary working lives.

The War on Terrorism will force the United States to carefully adjust its strategy to fit changing and unexpected conditions. The United States must also consider the effect its operations have on the rest of the world. If America is seen as a powerful bully that ignores the public interest in foreign nations, it will lose the cooperation of allies. The War on Terrorism, therefore, represents not just a military and police war, but also a public opinion war, a fight for sympathy and support around the world. Without such support the chances for success, and the prevention of future attacks such as those of September 11, will fade away.

☆ Chapter 1 ☆

Counterterrorism Abroad

The events of September 11 inspired sympathy around the world, even from traditionally unfriendly nations such as Pakistan and Iran. Newspapers carried banner headlines describing the attacks. Television stations played videotape of the two planes crashing into the World Trade Center, of the buildings collapsing, and of the destruction at the Pentagon. In London, Paris, Warsaw, and many other capitals, thousands of people marched in the streets, held candlelight vigils, and laid flowers at the front gates of American embassies.

In the days that followed, nearly every country in the world contacted President George W. Bush or his administration by telephone or through diplomatic messengers. These nations sent messages of condolence to Bush and to the United States. Many offered to cooperate with the United States in fighting terrorism.

This cooperation is much needed. The United States cannot enforce its own laws within the borders of another country. It cannot freely send military units or police agents across international borders. Federal agencies, such as the FBI and the CIA, must cooperate with foreign governments in order to get information on the identities and whereabouts of individual terrorists that might be hiding within their borders. The United States also needs the help of foreign governments to arrest terrorists and bring them to trial, either abroad or in the United States. Foreign armies, navies, and air forces can take part in military campaigns, allowing the United States to avoid "going it alone" when attacking a hostile nation.

Allies in the Fight

The most important group of allied countries in the War on Terrorism are the members of the powerful military alliance known as the North Atlantic Treaty Organization, or NATO. Formed immediately after World War II, NATO now includes the

United States, Belgium, Canada, Denmark, France, Great Britain, Iceland, Italy, Luxembourg, Netherlands, Norway, Portugal, Greece, Turkey, Germany, Spain, the Czech Republic, Hungary, and Poland.

The NATO nations acted quickly to assist the United States after September 11. The members held an emergency meeting and invoked Article 5 of their founding treaty. This article states that an attack on one NATO country will be considered an attack on all. These countries pledged their military forces in the War on Terrorism that had just been declared by President Bush. These forces first saw action in the U.S.-led campaign against the Taliban government of Afghanistan, which began a few weeks after the September 11 attacks.

A crowd outside the U.S. Embassy in Paris, France, honors the victims of the September 11 terrorist attacks.

For several reasons, Great Britain has been the most supportive NATO ally in the War on Terrorism. The British have a long history in Afghanistan, the home of al-Qaeda and its leader, Osama bin Laden. The British willingly share information from their own intelligence sources in Afghanistan with the Central Intelligence Agency (CIA), the most important U.S. intelligence agency working abroad. The British also have contributed their own ground troops and air force in ground campaigns in Afghanistan and Iraq.

Other NATO allies make important military contributions in Afghanistan. Canadian Special Operations forces still take part in missions against suspected terrorist hideouts, and Canadian Air Force planes carried out airlift and cargo flights within Afghanistan. Engineers from Poland helped rebuild airfields and clear minefields around the Bagram Air Base in Afghanistan. After the ground campaign ended, Germany flew a large force of peacekeepers to Afghanistan and helped to set up and train a new Afghan police force.

Although the government of France opposes some aspects of the War on Terrorism, France still assists the United States in a variety of ways. French infantry were on the ground in Afghanistan in the fall of 2001, and French aircraft based on carriers in the north Arabian Sea flew hundreds of reconnaissance missions. More than four thousand French officers and enlisted men remain in Afghanistan, and French cargo planes help with airdrops of humanitarian assistance—food, tents, clothing, and medical supplies.

Allies in the fight against terrorism come from outside of NATO as well. Several nations, including Albania and Kyrgyzstan, cooperated in Afghanistan operations by allowing NATO aircraft the right to fly over their territories. In Afghanistan, Bulgaria contributed heavy construction equipment as well as a forty-member decontamination team to inspect suspected chemical and biological weapons sites within Afghanistan. One of the most strategic non-NATO allies in Afghanistan has been Uzbekistan, a country that borders Afghanistan to the north.

Article 5

The following is the text of Article 5 of the North Atlantic Treaty, which was put into effect on April 4, 1949. This clause was invoked by NATO members after the terrorist attacks of September 11 (the complete treaty text is available online at NATO's website).

> The Parties agree that an armed attack against one or more of them in Europe or North America shall be considered an attack against them all and consequently they agree that, if such an armed attack occurs, each of them, in exercise of the right of individual or collective self-defense recognized by article 51 of the Charter of the United Nations, will assist the Party or Parties so attacked by taking forthwith, individually and in concert with the other Parties, such action as it deems necessary, including the use of armed force, to restore and maintain the security of the North Atlantic area.

A crew chief guides an American transport plane at an Uzbekistan airport.

An Ally in Central Asia

Uzbekistan has been cooperating in the U.S. effort against terrorism since well before September 11. During the 1990s Uzbekistan made military and political alliances with NATO and the United States. Uzbekistan also allowed the CIA to operate within its borders in the search for Osama bin Laden. After September 11 Uzbekistan agreed to let the United States use Uzbek military bases, including an airfield at Khanabad, near the Afghan border, as a jumping-off point for U.S. troops and planes fighting in the plains of northern Afghanistan. Uzbekistan also allowed the CIA to fly the Predator aircraft, an unmanned plane that carries an air-to-ground missile, from its territory. The United States also conducted search-and-rescue operations in low-flying helicopters to retrieve downed American pilots during the campaign in Afghanistan.

The Afghan ground campaign was conducted largely from Khanabad and other points in southern Uzbekistan. After the victory over the Taliban in the fall of 2001, Uzbekistan also agreed to serve as a staging ground for the International Security Assistance Force, or ISAF. These NATO-led forces were sent to stabilize Afghanistan, to support the government that replaced the Taliban, and to supply food, medicine, and humanitarian assistance to the people of Afghanistan.

Uzbekistan has its own motives for cooperating in the War on Terrorism. The president of Uzbekistan, Islam Karimov, wants closer relations with the United States. Karimov also seeks American help in his own struggle against the Islamic Movement of Uzbekistan (IMU), a group based in northern Afghanistan that is fighting to overthrow Karimov's government (in 2000 the IMU was officially categorized as a terrorist group by the United States). In the fall of 2001, Karimov wanted the United States to force the IMU out of its Afghan bases. Above all, Karimov wanted the Taliban government, which supported the IMU, eliminated.

In return for its cooperation, Uzbekistan has been offered a generous amount of financial aid by the United States. The U.S. military has trained and equipped Uzbek military and police forces. In a part of the world long troubled by civil and religious strife, Uzbekistan benefits from the stability that comes with a close financial, political, and military friendship with the world's most powerful country.

Intelligence Agencies

NATO and non-NATO allies also help American military and police fight the War on Terrorism. But America's national police agency, the Federal Bureau of Investigation (FBI), had little experience in fighting foreign terrorism before September 11. In addition, the FBI rarely cooperated with the Central Intelligence Agency, and neither had much to do with the National Security Agency (NSA). Counterterrorism on foreign soil demands an entirely new way of thinking and new plans of operation for all of these agencies.

For many years, the CIA did not have the resources, or the agents, to effectively deal with foreign terrorist groups. Several times prior to September 11, the agency had tried to find Osama bin Laden and infiltrate his organization, but found it to be a near impossible task. Al-Qaeda is made up mostly of young, fervently religious Muslim men. Infiltrating that group was nearly impossible for a largely non-Arab, non-Muslim CIA staff of American male and female agents. Similarly, getting al-Qaeda members to turn against bin Laden proved difficult because al-Qaeda ties are largely familial and religious—members are not likely to break these powerful connections. As author Bill Gertz explains in his book *Breakdown: The Failure of American Intelligence to Defeat Global Terror*, the CIA failed to adequately investigate and prevent terrorist activity:

> By July 1996, the CIA had no one close to bin Laden, . . . the CIA, FBI, and other intelligence agencies had adopted the high-technology approach to gathering information; but these agencies significantly lacked "human intelligence" from people in a position to know the plans and activities of al Qaeda. By 1996, when bin Laden began launching spectacular and deadly attacks, the U.S. intelligence

A Controversial Policy

The alliance of the United States with Uzbekistan during the campaign in Afghanistan was loudly criticized outside of the United States. Many people believe that the United States, while claiming to fight for democracy and freedom, hypocritically supports tyrannical governments that help advance U.S. interests in the rest of the world. Others accuse the United States of trying to establish control over smaller, weaker nations. This opinion, very common in the Muslim world, was succinctly expressed by Imran Waheed, leader of the Uzbek organization Hizb ut-Tahrir, in his Web article "Egypt/Uzbekistan Crooked Partners in the 'War on Terrorism'": "It is undeniable that the real motive for waging 'War Against Terrorism' is not to counter terrorism. The real motive is clearly to establish and strengthen US hegemony [authority] and influence over the Islamic lands, their people, and their resources in order to repress any semblance of Islamic political resurgence."

community was effectively blind, deaf, and dumb.[2]

After September 11, the government made important changes in the ground rules for the CIA and its operations in foreign countries. On September 17, 2001, President Bush signed a Memorandum of Notification (MON), authorizing lethal covert action to disrupt terrorist networks. The CIA was allowed to use its own paramilitary teams, officers, agents, and the Predator drone inside Afghanistan. The objective was no secret: The president himself publicly announced that Osama bin Laden was wanted "dead or alive."

The FBI also has made some important changes in the way it operates. Traditionally, the FBI had only handled criminal and terrorist cases arising within the United States. It was originally founded to investigate crimes taking place across state lines, such as the bank-robbing sprees of the 1930s. Although the FBI employed listening devices to capture the planners of the first World Trade Center attack in 1993 and was successful in capturing Timothy McVeigh, who helped bomb the Alfred P. Murrah Federal Building in Oklahoma City, it has not had much experience dealing with terrorism cases.

To fight the War on Terrorism, the FBI has opened offices in foreign capitals and is working with foreign police departments to track suspects and gather information. The Foreign Terrorist Tracking Task Force (FTTTF), run from FBI headquarters in Washington, D.C., monitors several hundred individuals believed to be terrorists and attempts to prevent them from getting into the United States. In addition, a Counterterrorism Watch listens to communications around the world, identifies threats of immediate terrorist attacks, passes its information on to local police agencies, and reports daily to the president. A Document Exploitation Working Group (DocEx) analyzes seized evidence from around the world, such as documents and video and audiotapes, to gain insight into what plans terrorist groups may have.

FBI agents raid a house in New York to arrest five suspected al-Qaeda members.

To effectively combat terrorism, the FBI and CIA also must share their information. For decades, the two organizations were rivals, but after information came to light that the September 11 plot might have been uncovered had the two agencies shared evidence in their possession, they had to become partners. They also cooperate with the National Security Agency, a large organization that also had its own way of doing things.

The National Security Agency

Since September 11, the National Security Agency has become a key component of the War on Terrorism. The NSA is responsible for gathering and analyzing communications from foreign countries. The NSA is like a long-range antenna of the U.S. government; it listens for useful information from a variety of sources. French author Roland Jacquard in his book *In the Name of Osama Bin Laden: Global Terrorism and the Bin Laden Brotherhood* describes the NSA's functions as follows:

> The NSA has several thousand employees . . . in Arab countries who maintain permanent surveillance over the air waves with fixed and mobile listening systems. Filters using keywords make it possible for . . . computers to make a preliminary selection from the [crowded] air waves. . . . Words such as jihad, missiles, chemical weapons, or names of people can automatically activate recorders.[3]

Bullets and bombs are ineffective against terrorism when it is not known who the terrorists are, what they are planning to do, or where and when they are planning to do it. The key weapon against a terrorist attack is advance knowledge of it, which requires the ability to intercept and interpret terrorists' cell phone, satellite phone, and e-mail communications from among the billions of messages sent daily by people all around the globe. Intelligence agencies use such technology to locate terrorists and learn of their plans before they are able to carry out attacks.

The NSA also has a photo intelligence division, which uses images from satellite cameras positioned over the earth. The satellites can be maneuvered over any spot on Earth, and can transmit accurate and detailed images from as high as two hundred and fifty miles. A vehicle can be followed, training camps can be spotted, and weapons detected in places where outsiders on the ground are prevented from prying. The NSA's satellite images also provide a vital targeting weapon for bombing runs carried out by conventional air forces.

New innovations in intelligence gathering by the NSA and other agencies could bring important victories in the War on Terrorism. Anthony Lake describes these innovations in his book *Six Nightmares: Real*

The War on Terrorism Begins

It was early in the morning, just after 9 A.M. on September 11, 2001, when a visiting celebrity, President George W. Bush, took his seat at the front of a class at the Emma Booker Elementary School in Sarasota, Florida. The president was listening to and following a reading exercise as the teacher gave instructions and the attentive students gave their answers.

Suddenly, Andrew Card, one of the president's aides, walked up to the president and whispered something into his ear. He stopped listening to the teacher and her students. Card had told the president, "America is under attack."

Two passenger jetliners had been hijacked and deliberately flown into the Twin Towers of the World Trade Center in New York City. Another plane crashed into the Pentagon, the headquarters of the Department of Defense, in Washington, D.C. A fourth plane, its target unknown, crashed in rural Pennsylvania soon after the hijackers were overcome by the passengers. Over the next two hours, the Twin Towers in New York collapsed and more than three thousand were dead.

It was September 11, 2001, and the War on Terrorism had just begun.

Threats in a Dangerous World and How America Can Meet Them:

> Information operations could include gaining control over an enemy's decision-making process and cycle, and exploiting his data or communications systems without his knowledge. They also require protecting one's own computer and communications systems from intrusion, disruption, and destruction. The United States already has begun to explore this new terrain through new units like the army's Land Information Warfare Activity, or LIWA . . . [which] provides small field-support teams—including specialists in information security, computer security, military deception, psychological operations, and command-and-control targeting—to bolster a battlefield commander's primary staff in planning operations.[4]

Unconventional Warfare

But to be effective, the intelligence-gathering job of the CIA, FBI, and NSA also must be coordinated with military operations. The conventional forces of the United States include the Army, Navy, Marines, and Air Force. These organizations also include special forces groups, which are trained to carry out specific and very specialized tasks. Overall, the task of the military has usually been to fight a conventional war meant to capture or defend territory against a declared enemy.

Foreign counterterrorism efforts, however, demand something entirely different from the conventional armed forces of the United States. After September 11, military leaders scrambled to come up with a new means of fighting an enemy that does not seek to conquer territory, that does not wear a uniform, and that will not sign a peace treaty. This effort resulted in the "Afghan Model," which can be used for U.S. military action against governments in other parts of the world. This strategy combines special forces units on the ground and precision bombing and other air operations, including satellite reconnaissance and electronic eavesdropping. The military will also make use of local insurgencies or political opposition movements within the country where the military operates. These rebels become surrogate fighters who will, in theory, replace large numbers of conventional American infantry troops. Writer Stephen Biddle bluntly describes this precarious alliance: "Even ragtag local militias will suffice as allies."[5] In Afghanistan, however, even the Afghan Model was not a complete success. The enemy quickly adapted to the offensive tactics and had to be confronted by masses of American troops on the ground. As a result, military strategists have concluded that the Afghan Model may not succeed in future ground wars in the War on Terrorism.

The question of the proper military approach remains open as the War on Terrorism progresses. Many American politicians caution against relying too much on military force, fearing it will tarnish America's image

A U.S. Navy SEAL in eastern Afghanistan provides cover for his team as they advance on al-Qaeda and Taliban positions.

and jeopardize its relationship with its allies. Says Senator John McCain:

> I agree that we will have to use force wisely to avoid inflaming the hatred for America that our enemies have been allowed to sow in the Islamic world. Toward that end, we should try hard to minimize noncombatant casualties. If we can use means other than force in some countries to achieve our goal, then we should. But we must keep our attention firmly fixed on our primary goal. . . . We should use no more force than necessary, but no less than necessary. Fighting this war in half measures will only give our enemies time and opportunity to strike us again.[6]

Most military leaders believe that local conditions, which will vary in each country, must dictate the right approach. Senator McCain's advice, that civilian casualties must be minimized, is also an important consideration for the military and its relationship with countries around the world. In the future, it is clear that the War on Terrorism will be a cooperative effort between law enforcement and military operations, as well as between the nations that the United States counts as allies.

☆ Chapter 2 ☆

Targeting Sponsor States

Shortly after September 11, President George W. Bush issued a comprehensive statement about the U.S. position on countries that sponsor terrorism. This statement, called the Bush Doctrine, said that any nation that sponsors or harbors terrorist organizations would become a target of U.S. retaliation. The United States would consider these nations enemies and would either peacefully or violently force them to change their ways. In the War on Terrorism, the nations of the world would have to choose sides, and sponsoring terrorism would be unacceptable.

Bush made himself exceedingly clear in a speech delivered to a joint session of the U.S. Congress on September 20, 2001, when he announced:

> We will starve terrorists of funding, turn them one against another, drive them from place to place, until there is no refuge or no rest. And we will pursue nations that provide aid or safe haven to terrorism. Every nation, in every region, now has a decision to make. Either you are with us, or you are with the terrorists. From this day forward, any nation that continues to harbor or support terrorism will be regarded by the United States as a hostile regime.[7]

This statement implies that the War on Terrorism is a true world war. Every nation is defined in this war as an enemy or a friend of the United States.

Defining Enemies

The U.S. Department of State keeps an official list of countries that it believes sponsors terrorism. As of 2003, the list includes Cuba, Iran, Iraq, Libya, North Korea, Sudan, and Syria. Since 1993, no state has ever been removed or added to the "sponsor list." According to an official statement of the Department of State,

> The US Government has a long memory and will not simply expunge a terrorist's record because time has passed. The states that choose to harbor terrorists are like accomplices who provide shelter for criminals. They will be held accountable for their "guests'" actions. International terrorists should know, before they contemplate a crime, that they cannot hunker down in safe haven for a period of time and be absolved of their crimes.[8]

A foreign nation can sponsor terrorism in many different ways. The state may provide shelter to the members of a terrorist group or allow it to operate in the open. The state may provide money and weapons to the group and help it to plan attacks in other countries. The state may also provide "political cover," meaning it will explain or excuse the actions of the group by describing it as a legitimate political struggle carried out by means of violence.

The Bush administration charged that there was no difference between terrorists and those who sheltered or aided them, and thus, sponsor states became a focal point of the War on Terrorism. These enemy states are targeted with political, military, or economic measures that the United States hopes will convince them to become allies instead of foes.

Ayatollah Khomeini waves to supporters after returning to Iran from exile in 1979.

Sponsoring Terrorist Groups

One of the ways countries sponsor terrorism is by providing full support for terrorist groups around the world. Iran stands at the top of the U.S. government's list of states that engage in this practice. Iran has been a homeland of Middle Eastern terrorism and of fundamentalist Islam, the worldview that favors strict Islamic government in Muslim countries and opposition to the West, particularly to the American government. The United States has used political and economic weapons in an effort to end Iranian support for terrorism.

The conflict between the United States and Iran dates to 1979, when the Ayatollah Khomeini, the head of Iran's religious community of Shiite Muslims, led an Islamic revolution that overthrew the shah (ruler) of Iran. The Islamic revolution in Iran was inspirational for those seeking to create fundamentalist Islamic regimes elsewhere in the Muslim world. These sympathizers understood for the first time that it was possible to achieve full political power in a modern nation based on principles they believed in: rejection of Western culture, the use of sharia (Islamic) law, and government led by religious leaders rather than secular politicians.

Iran has been actively "exporting" its Islamic revolution by supporting terrorist groups operating in foreign countries. Most importantly, Iran sponsors and arms a group known as the Hizballah, which has been active in the strife-torn Middle Eastern nation of Lebanon since the 1980s. Hizballah, which means "Party of God," is a Lebanese group of Shiite Muslims who want to establish a fundamentalist state modeled on Iran. To this end, Hizballah bombers have attacked U.S. targets in Lebanon, including the U.S. embassy, and kidnapped and assassinated U.S. officials there. The group also carries out attacks on Israel, which lies along Lebanon's southern border.

Iran supports Hizballah militarily, financially, and politically. It sends guns, rockets, explosives, and other weaponry directly to the group, which turns these arms on its enemies in Lebanon and on cities and settlements in northern Israel. Iran provides training camps and business offices within Iran for Hizballah, and funnels money from Iranian contributors to the group through bank accounts in Iran. Certain factions of the Iranian government, including the country's intelligence service and its militant Revolutionary Guards, also cooperate with the leaders of Hizballah in Lebanon, while Iranian leaders lend words of support and encouragement to Hizballah and its fight against Israel.

Hizballah operates openly in Lebanon, and in many ways as an extension of Iran's government. Hizballah takes an active part in Lebanese political life, and Hizballah representatives sit in Lebanon's elected legislature. These representatives espouse Iran's viewpoint in Lebanon's internal debates and issues, and in Lebanon's relations with Israel and with Syria.

Syria and Libya

The nation of Syria also supports several terrorist groups, most of which fight against the

The Capture of the *Karine A*

In January 2002, Israeli naval forces captured the ship *Karine A* in the Mediterranean Sea. The ship was found to be carrying Katyusha rockets and long-range missiles. According to Israel, the weapons were meant for the Palestinian Authority, the government that legally represents the Palestinian Arabs. Investigators also discovered that the ship had been loaded at the Iranian island of Qeshm, and that the weapons had been sold to the Palestinian Authority by the government of Iran.

In the War on Terrorism, the capture of the *Karine A* was an important event, one that changed U.S. policy toward Iran. In the weeks after September 11, Iran and the United States had drawn closer on the diplomatic stage. A bitter enemy of the Taliban government of Afghanistan, the Iranian regime approved of the American war against the Taliban in November 2001. But the thawed relations grew cold again after the *Karine A* incident, when it was found that Iran was directly supporting military action against Israel, an ally of the United States in the Middle East.

Israeli navy forces seized these mortars and antitank missiles from the Karine A *(seen in background).*

state of Israel. These groups include Hamas, a Palestinian group that carries out suicide bombings within Israel, and Hizballah, which operates training camps in the Bekáa Valley of Lebanon, an area that Syria has controlled since the Lebanese civil war of the 1980s. Syria has shipped rockets to Hizballah, which launches these weapons against settlements in northern Israel. Syria also allows Iranian money and weapons destined for Hizballah to pass through its territory, and allows Hizballah to operate openly out of offices in the Syrian capital of Damascus.

The North African state of Libya is yet another sponsor of terrorism. Libya and its leader, Muammar Qaddafi, have given shelter, arms, and money to a variety of terrorist organizations, not only Middle Eastern or Arab groups. These include the Irish Republican Army, the Basque separatist group ETA, and the Revolutionary United Front, a group fighting in the African nation of Sierra Leone. The arms are either shipped directly to the groups or sent through Libyan embassies, which can send banned material across international borders in diplomatic

Hundreds of thousands of demonstrators in Damascus, Syria, protest the war in Iraq.

pouches, which are safe from search and seizure.

Libyan financial support of terrorist groups takes several forms. The Libyan government has collected taxes from Palestinian workers within Libya and sent the money to Palestinian terrorist groups. Libya has also paid money to groups that successfully carry out terrorist attacks. Libyan banks are depositories for money that terrorist groups use to pay for arms and explosives. Author John Pynchon Holmes lists some of Libya's involvements in his book *Terrorism: Today's Biggest Threat to Freedom:*

> Tripoli [the Libyan capital] frequently passes money to terrorists who train in-country. Virtually all terrorist operatives who are trained in Libya receive, at a minimum, travel money and a stipend for expenses. Libyan People's Bureaus and the Anti-Imperialism Centers are used to transfer funds for terrorists. Radical Palestinian groups often receive Libyan funding through bank accounts, particularly in the Middle East. On rare occasions the Libyans have used couriers to deliver money to terrorist organizations; the transfer usually occurs in a third country.[9]

The Libyan government also shelters terrorists on the run from criminal prosecution in other countries. Libyan diplomats set up safe houses for terrorists on foreign soil and also pass along information on possible targets for bombing, kidnapping, and assassination to would-be terrorists. Within its own borders, Libya has also set up training camps for terrorist groups and has helped these groups recruit new members among the general Libyan population.

Providing Weapons and Training

Fidel Castro, who took power in Cuba in 1959, is another leader who supports many revolutionary movements in Latin America and Africa by providing weapons and training for guerrilla fighters. For this reason, the United States put Cuba on its list of sponsor states. Much like Syria, Cuba's response has been that it supports legitimate political movements, whose success sometimes requires the use of terrorist tactics such as bombing, assassination, and kidnapping.

U.S. investigators, both civilian and military, are not convinced that Cuba has ties to terrorist groups that directly attack the United States, however. Nor does the United States consider Cuba itself a direct threat. Instead, the United States simply claims that Cuba offers shelter to foreign terrorists and protects them from standing trial in their home countries. These include members of the Basque separatist group Fatherland and Liberty (ETA), who face charges in

A Prison in Cuba

The United States and Cuba have been rivals since 1959, when Communist guerrilla leader Fidel Castro took power there. But Cuba is also the site of a U.S. military installation at Guantánamo Bay, which was built before Castro's revolution and which the United States did not abandon. Here the United States has gathered about 675 prisoners from the War on Terrorism. Most of them are members of the Taliban and other men suspected of belonging to al-Qaeda.

The prisoners are kept at a detention center known as Camp X-Ray, where they are locked in small cages made of concrete and chainlink fence topped with razor wire. All go through interrogations and some will be put on trial as war criminals. Some international organizations, including the International Red Cross, have protested these conditions and demand that the United States follow the Geneva Convention, an international agreement on the treatment of prisoners of war. The United States, however, believes the prisoners are illegal combatants and should not have the rights of ordinary soldiers taken prisoner.

Spain, and members of the Revolutionary Armed Forces of Colombia (FARC), a group fighting a longstanding guerrilla war in that South American nation.

The United States has also named North Korea a sponsor of global terrorism since 1979. North Korea, according to the United States, supplies terrorist groups and sponsor states around the world with arms much more dangerous than guns. North Korea has admitted that it is attempting to make nuclear weapons. North Korea has also developed several types of long-range missiles, including the Taepodong-2 missile, which has a range of almost twenty-two hundred miles—far enough to reach the state of Alaska.

The United States wants to head off the North Korean nuclear program at all costs. To convince North Korea that it should halt the program, the United States has extended promises of financial and technical aid to the North Korean government. But North Korea has stubbornly refused to keep to agreements to halt its nuclear program. If North Korea succeeds in building nuclear-tipped missiles, the North Korean government may sell these weapons to terrorist groups, who are not yet capable of building the weapons on their own. North Korea already sells missile technology to other nations that the United States designates as sponsors of terrorism, such as Iran, Syria, and Libya.

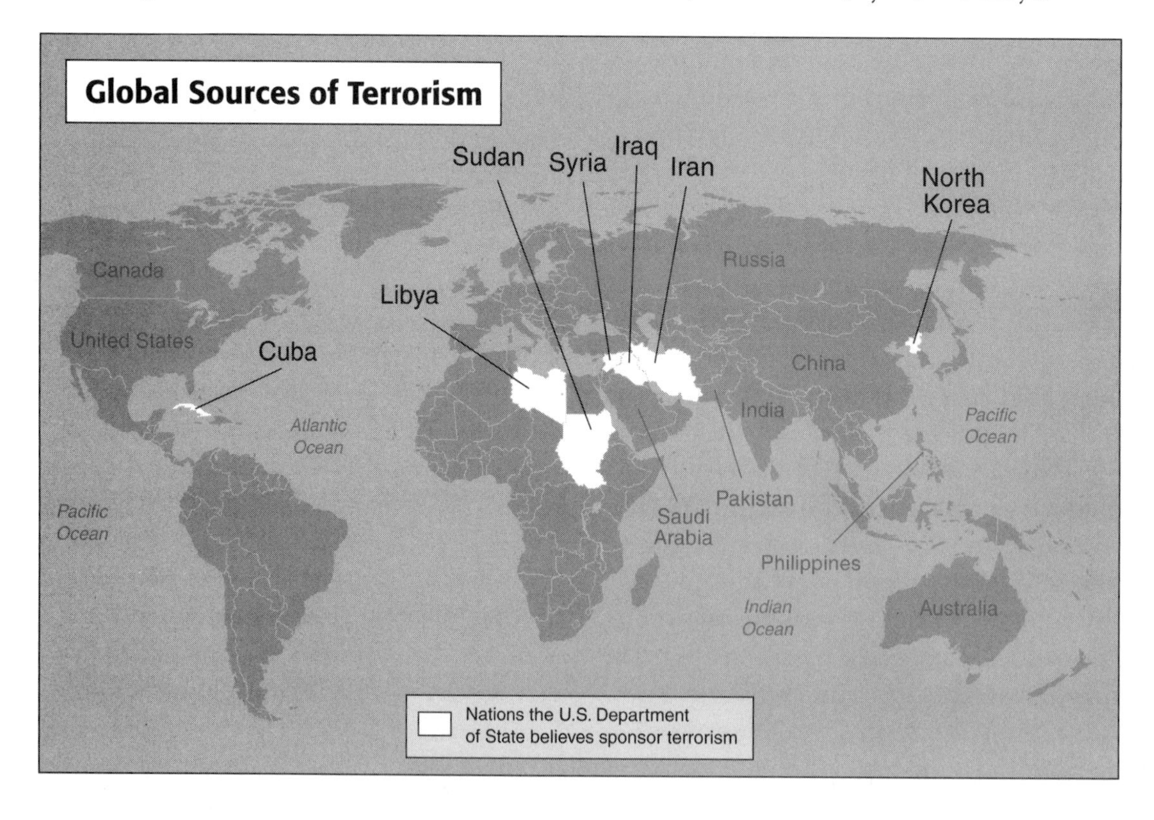

Providing a Base

Still another way that states support terrorism is to allow terrorist groups to establish training camps and military bases on their territory. From such bases, terrorist attacks can be planned and carried out. For example, Sudan, a desperately poor and war-torn nation of northeastern Africa, has allowed al-Qaeda and other terrorist organizations to establish headquarters and training camps there. These groups have been supported by the National Islamic Front, the Islamic party that controls Sudan. Al-Qaeda made its headquarters in Sudan from 1991 until it was expelled in 1996. From their Sudan base Osama bin Laden and his lieutenants planned and carried out several major terrorist operations, including simultaneous bombings of two American embassies, in Kenya and Tanzania, in 1998. In addition, Sudan has harbored members of the Abu Nidal international terrorist group, the Egyptian group Islamic Jihad, as well as Hizballah and Hamas.

More recently, the fundamentalist Taliban regime of Afghanistan gave shelter and support to Osama bin Laden. After bin Laden was expelled from Sudan, he moved his headquarters to the mountainous and isolated nation, which assured him political and physical safety. At the time of the 2001 attacks on the United States, al-Qaeda operated more than a dozen separate camps in Afghanistan. Bin Laden used these camps to enlist and train members from the Middle East, Africa, and Asia. The recruits lived in primitive conditions while learning how to handle weapons and explosives, how to maintain cover identities in foreign nations, and how to receive and follow instructions from al-Qaeda leaders. The camps were much like military bases, which kept outsiders at bay and forged a sense of camaraderie and a common goal to those who found acceptance inside.

Although the United States attacked these camps with cruise missiles and sent Predator aircraft over the country in the search for bin Laden, these operations failed to root out al-Qaeda or kill its leader. Nor did political pressure have any effect on the Taliban, a political party that imposed a fundamentalist Islamic regime and paid little heed to diplomatic or economic pressure imposed by foreign nations.

The U.S. effort against the Taliban changed dramatically after September 11, when Afghanistan found itself the first nation to be subjected to the Bush Doctrine. The country was attacked by U.S. planes and invaded from the north by U.S. ground troops fighting alongside Afghan opponents of the Taliban. In about a month, the campaign destroyed the Taliban regime, sending Taliban and al-Qaeda leaders fleeing into remote areas of the neighboring country of Pakistan.

State Terrorist Operations

In addition to financing and equipping terrorist groups, some sponsor states, such as Libya, have also carried out terrorist actions on their own. In 1986 Libyan agents bombed the La Belle discotheque in Berlin, Germany,

A British helicopter flies above the crash site of Pan Am Flight 103 in Lockerbie, Scotland.

an act that killed three people, including two American soldiers. The most famous act of Libyan state terrorism was the bombing of Pan Am Flight 103 over Lockerbie, Scotland, in 1988. The plane exploded above the small Scottish town, killing 270 people on board and on the ground. According to investigators, the bomb that destroyed Pan Am Flight 103 was assembled and placed on the aircraft by two Libyan government agents.

After several years of diplomatic haggling, Libya surrendered the two accused agents to an international criminal court in the Netherlands. In 2001 this court convicted Abdel Basset Ali al-Megrahi of carrying out the bombing of Flight 103 and found the other agent innocent. In the summer of 2003, Libya publicly admitted that its government played a role in the bombing.

The United States uses a variety of methods to combat this type of state sponsorship of terrorism. These methods include economic punishment, diplomatic maneuvering, and outright threats. In deciding which method to use, the government must take into account a unique set of circumstances in each nation. While some nations are vulnerable to trade sanctions that threaten their economic well-being, others can be persuaded through diplomacy. Still others are vulnerable to revolutionary movements that threaten the government in power. The most important and effective weapon in the War on Terrorism since 2001, however, has been financial punishment, which takes many different forms.

Economic Warfare

When a country makes the terrorist sponsor state list, the U.S. government declares economic war against that country. American businesses are banned from conducting certain kinds of trade—and in many cases, Congress has passed laws banning *all* normal trade—with a terrorist sponsor state. The country is not eligible for loans, either through government programs or through private businesses. If the target state keeps money or owns property in the United States, those assets may be frozen, meaning they cannot be sold or removed. The strategy behind such laws and sanctions is to isolate sponsor states and cause them to suffer economically until they stop supporting terrorist groups.

The United States put an economic strategy in place against North Korea during the 1990s. Consequently, American companies cannot deal with North Korea in any way. They may not buy North Korean goods, nor may they sell their own goods in that country. This strategy is believed to be effective because North Korea is desperately poor and is struggling to survive. It has little money in its public treasury and few goods to trade with the outside world (other than weapons). If North Korea gives up its weapons program altogether the United States promises to lift the sanctions.

In 1996 the United States as well as the United Nations also imposed sanctions on Sudan in an attempt to persuade its government to completely renounce terrorism. The UN lifted its sanctions in 2001 but the United States did not. This did not prevent Sudan from providing shelter to al-Qaeda members after the war in Afghanistan in the fall of 2001. During the war al-Qaeda sent men (as well as money) into Sudan to protect them from American troops and investigators.

After the September 11 attacks, however, Sudan did take some steps under pressure from the United States. The government of Sudan declared its opposition to terrorism in hopes of escaping the sanctions already imposed and new ones threatened by the United States. Sudan has cooperated with American investigators, tracking al-Qaeda members and money.

The United States has, in turn, tried to negotiate a cease-fire in the Sudanese civil war. The United States pursues peace negotiations in this distant country because it believes an end to the civil war would also encourage Sudan to end its support of terrorist groups. If Sudan achieves peace within its borders, its government may want to cut all ties to terrorists in order to gain diplomatic recognition and financial aid from foreign nations, including the United States.

Economic pressure has also had some results in Libya. For many years, the bombing of Pan Am Flight 103 kept Libya on the state sponsor list and prevented normal economic and diplomatic relations between Libya and the United States. Nevertheless, General Qaddafi wants Western businesses to invest in his country and knows that support of terrorism prevents it. During the late 1990s Libya closed terrorist training camps operating within its borders and expelled the Abu Nidal terrorist group, which then took refuge in Iraq. In an attempt to improve relations with the United States, Qaddafi expressed support for the United States after the attacks of September 11 and ordered his government to share information on groups and individuals with ties to al-Qaeda.

Qaddafi continues to claim that his country is innocent in the matter of terrorism. In his own words, spoken to a CNN journalist,

> As a matter of fact, actually, we are only the victims of terrorism and Libya is against terrorism. . . . I'd like also to reassure the Americans and non-Americans that Libya plays a very important role in combating and fighting terrorism. . . . Actually, we are not in need of bin Laden. . . . We don't need his money, we don't need his protection, we don't want to use him or be used by him. We just want to defend ourselves.[10]

Despite Qaddafi's assurances, the United States still believes his country supports terror. The U.S. government has therefore maintained economic pressure on Libya, and even bars U.S. citizens from traveling there or conducting any business with Libya. The economic pressure, U.S. officials hope, will finally convince Qaddafi to completely renounce all forms of terrorism in the Middle East and elsewhere.

Supporting Political Change

Another method of punishing states that support terror is to push for political change within those countries or topple the ruling governments altogether. The wars in both Afghanistan and Iraq were fought to this end. In 2003 the Bush administration sent a similar message to the fundamentalist government of Iran. The United States wants to see a second Iranian revolution, in which the clerics give up their authority and a new

Iran and the U.S. in Iraq

While the United States struggled to constitute a new Iraqi government after the fall of the Saddam Hussein regime, Iran took a strong interest in the events. Determined to have influence in the new government, Iran backed the Supreme Council for Islamic Revolution in Iraq, or SCIRI, a party made up of Iraqis who adhere to the Shiite Islam that is prevalent in Iran. This party strongly opposed American plans for the new Iraqi government. In the weeks after the war in Iraq, SCIRI members carried out violent demonstrations against the American occupation.

The United States and Iran have had a very hostile relationship since the Iranian revolution of 1979. Despite Iran's public condemnation of the September 11 attacks, the United States believes that many al-Qaeda members took shelter in Iran after their defeat in Afghanistan. The United States also criticizes Iranian "meddling" in Iraqi affairs, saying that Iran is prompting Iraqi Shiites to fight U.S. authority. If such diplomatic conflict continues, the United States may threaten Iran with outright invasion and conquest.

government, more sympathetic to the West and to the United States, takes power. In order to encourage this change, the United States supports reformist politicians in Iran who oppose the present Iranian government.

The United States believes that a reformist victory is possible. Iran has suffered in many ways since the Islamic revolution. The people are poor, and many are unhappy with Iran's Islamic government. After the 1979 revolution Iran cut most of its cultural and economic ties with the West. Now a significant portion of its population, especially younger people, wish to restore these ties.

To help bring about a change in government, the United States supports moderate political groups within Iran. It does not want to intervene militarily, however. If Iran is seen as the victim of an American war, moderate groups will be accused of allying themselves with the United States. In the same way, any outright attack on Cuba would be seen as an act of aggression against a much smaller and weaker neighbor, one not considered by anybody as a threat to the United States.

Diplomacy

Finally, the United States and its allies use diplomacy as a way of discouraging states from supporting terror. American diplomats sometimes do this by presenting issues to the United Nations, where they may propose UN sanctions and resolutions against countries that sponsor terrorism. Diplomatic alliances with the target countries' neighbors and enemies are sometimes formed. Treaties may also be negotiated to pursuade errant nations to help, rather than hinder, the global military and police effort against terrorism.

Diplomacy has been enacted to attempt to curb North Korea's nuclear program and prevent it from arming terrorist groups with weapons of mass destruction. In 1994 the United States and North Korea signed an important treaty, which stated that North Korea would stop its nuclear weapons program. In return, the United States would supply North Korea with technology that would allow it to pursue peaceful uses of nuclear power, including the generation of electricity. North Korea violated this treaty by continuing its weapons program in secret, however, a fact that it admitted in 2002.

A more useful strategy at work against North Korea is known as triangle diplomacy. The United States and China, North Korea's neighbor and only ally, are working together to pressure the North Korean government to give up its pursuit of nuclear weapons. If North Korea loses its alliance with China, it will become completely isolated, without a single political or military friend in the world. Despite these strategies, the standoff between the United States and North Korea remains stubbornly in place. North Korea repeatedly threatens to arm itself with nuclear weapons and declares that it has the right to use these weapons against a U.S. attack. The United States, in turn, refuses to extend financial aid to North Korea and insists that North Korea follow its treaty obligations.

When economic and diplomatic strategies fail, the United States is left with few weapons other than an outright military attack. After September 2001, this strategy was employed in Afghanistan, and the success of the campaign beginning in October 2001, which destroyed the Taliban government, provided a model for what many believe will become the standard of warfare in the twenty-first century.

Chapter 3

Providing a Model: Afghanistan

After identifying al-Qaeda as the group responsible for the September 11 attacks, the United States declared the War on Terrorism and turned its attention to Afghanistan, a mountainous nation of central Asia. Afghanistan had been al-Qaeda's haven since May 1996, when the Afghan government, known as the Taliban, offered al-Qaeda's leader Osama bin Laden shelter and military support. Al-Qaeda training camps operated in remote areas of the mountainous country. Recruits trained there came from all over the world—from the Middle East, North Africa, Europe, Indonesia, and the Philippines. About one thousand members of the Arab Brigade, an elite wing of the Taliban military, also trained in al-Qaeda camps.

President Bush demanded that the Taliban government expel al-Qaeda and turn over Osama bin Laden. This demand, according to author Peter L. Bergen, clashed with an important cultural tradition among the Afghan ethnic and tribal group known as Pathans, who offer shelter to all those who ask for refuge, no matter how serious the accusation against them:

> The Taliban leadership subscribe to the ancient and elaborate Pathan tribal code of conduct, pukhtunwali. Pukhtunwali puts an enormous premium on two concepts: malmastiya, "the obligation to show hospitality to all visitors . . ." and nanawati, the offering of asylum. . . . The Taliban finds handing over bin Laden as unimaginable as a Christian priest in the Middle Ages would have found it to hand over someone who had sought sanctuary in his church.[11]

The Taliban refused the request of the United States. Because Afghanistan was already isolated both diplomatically and economically from the rest of the world, trade sanctions and diplomacy could not change the Taliban's stance. Nor did the United States seem capable of uniting the Taliban's opponents to overthrow the government, as Afghanistan is composed of a patchwork of ethnic groups that have been contesting political power for centuries. The U.S. government saw no peaceful means of forcing the Taliban to cooperate, and so used military force to enforce the Bush Doctrine for the first time.

Military conquest, however, does not come easily in Afghanistan. The country is landlocked; there are few large cities or major roads, and communications with the outside world are poor. Conquerors have tried many times to subdue the nation to no avail. In the late 1980s, for example, Afghan mujahideen (guerrilla fighters) resisted an occupation by the Soviet Union, then a military superpower. In the 1990s the United States had no better luck fighting in Afghanistan, although they did so from a distance. The United States bombed al-Qaeda's Afghan camps after the African embassy attacks in 1998 and the bombing of the USS *Cole* in 2000, but did not harm Osama bin Laden and did very little to disrupt his organization. To destroy the Taliban and root out al-Qaeda in 2001, the U.S. military took a new approach to what military strategists call "asymmetric warfare," in which opponents use different tactics and fight with very different weapons.

The 1980s: Different Priorities

In the late 1970s, to fight the Soviet occupation of Afghanistan, President Jimmy Carter authorized the CIA to send money, arms, and fighters into Afghanistan through Pakistan. American support for the anti-Soviet fighters increased during the administration of President Ronald Reagan. The Reagan administration saw the rivalry with the Soviet Union—and not with fundamantalist Islam or terrorism—as being of paramount importance to U.S. interests.

One of the anti-Soviet fighters was Osama bin Laden, who arrived in Afghanistan from Saudi Arabia to take part in the battle. After the defeat of the Soviet Union in Afghanistan, bin Laden and many of his comrades formed al-Qaeda and took up a new mission: the end of U.S. influence in the Middle East.

A New Model of Warfare

This was to be the first battle of the War on Terrorism, and an important testing ground for new techniques of warfare, which military planners call the Afghan Model. If successful, the Afghan Model could be used in other places where small terrorist groups operate underground and employ stealth, disguise, and surprise rather than tanks, planes, and infantry.

In Afghanistan, conventional military forces coordinated with special forces and intelligence agencies (such as the CIA and the NSA), and fought alongside local Afghan militias. The intelligence agencies followed the Taliban army and located fixed targets, such as air defense systems, ammunition and fuel dumps, troop barracks, headquarters buildings, roads, bridges, and telephone exchanges, which the conventional military forces would destroy. Following the elimination of fixed targets, special forces units on the ground directed American pilots to "emerging" targets and enemy units that appeared as the situation changed on the ground.

Instead of set battles, in which masses of infantry and armored vehicles fight over cities and territory, the Afghan Model targeted individuals, particularly Osama bin Laden, and sought to disperse and capture a small group of enemies disguised as civilians. Instead of invading Afghanistan with tanks and troops, the United States employed small special forces teams as well as the Northern Alliance, the Taliban's most powerful opponents within Afghanistan. Paramilitary groups belonging to the CIA also worked with the Northern Alliance and with special forces units. Using this strategy, the Northern Alliance staged an advance from its bases in northern Afghanistan, captured the strategic town of Mazar-e Sharif from the Taliban, and soon overran the Afghan capital of Kabul.

The Public Relations War

The Bush administration considered the "public-relations war," that is, the effort to gain the support of neutral countries and the Afghan population, to be as important as the military operations. The United States did not want to be seen as a hostile invading force in Afghanistan. It did not want to cause civilian casualties, destroy villages, overrun cities, or create a famine. It wanted to persuade the Afghans that the United States was fighting to liberate them from their own tyrannical government. It wanted other nations to extend their help in the War on Terrorism, and not condemn it as a war of American aggression.

To achieve this, the military laid out very specific rules of engagement concerning collateral damage, or military action that causes civilian deaths and the destruction of civilian property. According to the rules, bombing that would probably not cause collateral damage could be carried out with only the approval of military leaders in the field. But if a bombing ran the risk of causing high collateral damage, Bush himself would have to approve the attack. The only exception to this rule was a proposed attack on bin Laden himself, which did not need advance approval.

The United States also employed psychological warfare, which was intended to intimidate the enemy and undermine their confidence. For example, the United States aired radio broadcasts to enemy fighters from airplanes flying over the country. One such American broadcast claimed:

> Our forces are armed with state of the art military equipment. What are you using, obsolete and ineffective weaponry? Our helicopters will rain fire down upon your camps before you detect them on your radar. Our bombs are so accurate we can drop them right through your windows. Our infantry is trained for any climate and terrain on earth. United States soldiers fire with superior marksmanship and are armed with superior weapons.

> You have only one choice. . . . Surrender now and we will give you a second chance. We will let you live.[12]

To gain support among Afghan civilians, the United States dropped millions of leaflets over their country. The leaflets described the war as a war of liberation and warned the people not to fight for the Taliban. They were instructed to flee areas near barracks, airfields, supply depots, and other military targets. The leaflets portrayed the conflict as an effort by native Afghans to rout the Arab outsiders, particularly Osama bin Laden, who had taken advantage of their country's hospitality.

To prevent the usual suffering of civilians in wartime, the United States also carried out airdrops of food and medicine. American pilots scattered huge bundles of small food packets over the Afghan countryside, a technique known as "snowdropping," allowing anyone within a large area to gather the food. Although some of these food packets made their way into civilian homes, much of it went instead to Taliban and al-Qaeda fighters, who claimed their share of humanitarian supplies at the point of a gun.

An Allied Effort

The United States was selling the war to a much larger audience than the Afghans, however. The Bush administration believed that the support of neutral nations, particularly those in Europe, was critical to future successes in the War on Terrorism. It also wanted the war to be seen as a coalition effort, one in which many nations outside the United States would take part. To this end, the United States appealed to these nations for both military and humanitarian aid in Afghanistan.

In response, Russia, Britain, and most of the Western European nations offered assistance to the United States in Afghanistan. Russia granted the United States the right to use its airspace for humanitarian airdrops. It also pledged assistance with search and rescue operations, in case any American pilots or soldiers were shot down over Afghanistan or captured by the Taliban. Russia also agreed to apply pressure on the central Asian republics to allow the U.S. military to set up bases on their territory.

Britain offered the use of special operations forces, and agreed to share intelligence gathered from its own agents in southern Afghanistan. France provided humanitarian aid in the form of medical supplies and doctors. Belgium delivered food packets as well as vaccinations for Afghan children. A hospital operated by Spanish doctors performed emergency surgeries and accommodated several thousand military and civilian patients.

Many of these nations were eager to help, but not willing to put their own military forces on the line. For the Bush administration, this stance was perfectly acceptable. Military leaders at the Pentagon did not want to involve large foreign military units in Afghanistan. They did not want American commanders bickering with for-

Civilians in northern Afghanistan collect humanitarian food packets dropped by U.S. aircraft.

eign officers over their proper authority on the battlefield. They did not want to coordinate the movements of several different national armies, each with its own uniforms, language, weaponry, tactics, and customs. They wanted to fight and win the war as quickly and efficiently as possible.

Victory in Afghanistan

For several weeks, the war in Afghanistan made halting, uncertain progress. Aerial bombing slowed; hundreds of targets had been destroyed, and new ones could not be found. The Taliban held their positions, and Kabul, the Afghan capital, remained under their control. Al-Qaeda moved its camps and hideouts to the more remote mountains of Afghanistan, places impossible to destroy from the air.

Then an important breakthrough occurred. The Northern Alliance, backed by American air power, captured the strategic city of Mazar-e Sharif in the north. This victory quickly drove the Taliban forces back into the capital of Kabul, which fell on November 13. The surviving members of the

The Usefulness of Technology

Discussing the Afghan Model of warfare in his article "Afghanistan and the Future of Warfare," author Stephen Biddle contends that advanced reconnaissance (that is, intelligence gathering) and aerial bombing does not always bring victory. Biddle points out that al-Qaeda fighters quickly adapted to the modern methods of the U.S. military, and in many places the war had to be fought the old-fashioned way: with ground troops using small arms. He describes one battle in which al-Qaeda and Taliban fighters were able to fight effectively despite thorough surveillance conducted by the U.S. military:

"How could such surprise be possible in an era of persistent reconnaissance drones, airborne radars, satellite surveillance, thermal imaging, and hypersensitive electronic eavesdropping equipment? The answer is that the earth's surface remains an extremely complex environment with an abundance of natural and manmade cover available for those militaries capable of exploiting it."

Taliban government and its leader, Mullah Mohammed Omar, retreated to the southern city of Kandahār. A group of al-Qaeda holdouts moved to the city of Kunduz, northeast of Mazar-e Sharif, where they surrendered on November 26.

With U.S. special forces fighting alongside the Southern Alliance led by the Afghan leader Hamid Karzai, the southern city of Kandahār then fell. The Taliban government disintegrated, and al-Qaeda members scattered to nearby Iran and Pakistan. The United States continued to bomb al-Qaeda hideouts in the heights of Tora Bora, a region of the White Mountains west of Kabul. Information from local people convinced the United States that Osama bin Laden himself was hiding out in the Tora Bora caves. Heavy bombing of this region continued for two weeks, while special forces troops searched caves and tunnels bored into the mountainsides.

The last phase of the military campaign, Operation Anaconda, took place in March 2002, long after the fall of Kabul and the Taliban government. This took place in the Shahi Kot Valley south of the town of Gardez. Al-Qaeda fighters were either killed or driven out of the Shahi Kot Valley and across the border into Pakistan. Others were thought to have left for Iraq, Syria, and Iran, three nations that are suspected of offering al-Qaeda members shelter and a chance to regroup.

In asymmetric warfare, the site of the fighting may quickly shift from countryside to city streets and back again, and intense fighting can be followed by a lull. Just such a lull in the campaign against al-Qaeda occurred after Operation Anaconda. During the rapid advance of the Northern Alliance after the fall of Mazar-e Sharif, the United States had overrun many al-Qaeda camps. In these camps U.S. troops and investigators found weapons and explosives as well as address books, laptop computers, videotapes, and telephones. Recorded on much of this equipment were the names and locations of hundreds of al-Qaeda fighters as well as vital contact information for al-

Qaeda supporters around the world. According to journalist David E. Kaplan, "Among the key finds: rosters of trainees at al Qaeda facilities, which gave the CIA a handle on the tens of thousands of jihadists [holy warriors] who had passed through some 50 camps across Afghanistan. 'They were like the Nazis,' says an FBI terror expert. 'They were meticulous record keepers.'"[13]

The valuable finds allowed the United States to continue pursuing al-Qaeda, even after the military chased the organization out of Afghanistan. The information was collected and sent back to CIA headquarters in the United States. CIA analysts translated and analyzed thousands of lists and documents. This allowed the organization to build a huge database of information on the identity and whereabouts of al-Qaeda members.

The United States would now turn the military campaign into a large-scale police investigation to hunt down and arrest surviving al-Qaeda members.

The Bonn Agreement and Postwar Problems

The stabilization of Afghanistan was another important nonmilitary battle to fight in the War against Terrorism. U.S. strategists believed that outsiders such as Osama bin Laden could not use Afghanistan as a terrorist headquarters in the

Battles for Afghanistan, November–December 2001

future if the country had a functioning government, a healthy economy, and satisfied citizens.

In December 2001, the Afghan factions took one small step toward stability with the Bonn Agreement. They agreed to a "road map," a plan that will end in a permanent, democratic government to replace the Taliban. Hamid Karzai was appointed as the new president of Afghanistan and the head of a twenty-nine-member interim council. In July 2003, Karzai appointed a traditional grand council, known as a Loya Jirga. The task of the five hundred members of the Loya Jirga was to write a new constitution. This document spells out the structure of the

Afghan president Hamid Karzai (seated at right) sits with Donald Rumsfeld during a press conference in Kabul.

government, the timing of elections, and the basic rights of Afghan citizens.

Inside Kabul, a five-thousand-member International Security Assistance Force (ISAF) began patrolling the streets. The ISAF includes troops from NATO and non-NATO countries. These soldiers, most of whom are German or Dutch, train a new Afghan police force, patrol important sites such as the airport and government buildings, and search for contraband arms and explosives. But the ISAF does not operate outside of Kabul. While the United States has several bases outside of the capital, its own zone of control in Afghanistan remains very limited. In many places there is a power vacuum, where control from Kabul and by the central government is nonexistent.

Private Militias and Warlords

In this power vacuum warlords control large areas of the countryside, and even some large cities. Their armed and well-organized private militias move about, fighting their enemies, smuggling arms and contraband, and demanding payment from local villagers and farmers for "protection." For this reason, the country remains unsafe and its future is very unclear. The most powerful of these warlords, Gulbuddin Hekmatyar, is the leader of the Hizb-e-Islami party. Hekmatyar works from a base in western Afghanistan and organizes attacks on U.S. troops, on the ISAF, on the interim government in Kabul, and on Hamid Karzai himself.

Hekmatyar's goal is to drive the United States and the ISAF completely out of Afghanistan. If successful, he intends to replace Karzai's government with an Islamist regime. He has declared a jihad, or holy war, against the American troops. Many al-Qaeda and Taliban fighters, dispersed throughout Afghanistan and Pakistan after the fall of 2001, are rallying to his cause.

The United States responded to Hekmatyar's campaign by giving him the same official status of "global terrorist" that Osama bin Laden has. Hekmatyar became one of the individuals sought "dead or alive" in the War on Terrorism. In May 2002, the United States tracked Hekmatyar to a mountain gorge near Kabul, attacked with a Hellfire missile launched from a Predator drone, and missed its target. As it continues the search, the U.S. government will seize Hekmatyar's assets in the United States, if any can be found. In addition, anyone who supports Hekmatyar in any way is subject to criminal prosecution by the U.S. government.

The reconstruction of Afghanistan has become an important part of the effort to make it stable. Two decades of war brought the destruction of homes, schools, office buildings, television and radio broadcasting equipment, electrical generating stations, water wells, hospitals, and roads and bridges. Soon after the fighting largely ceased in the fall of 2001, the United States and the United Nations began sending food, medicine, and clothing to the Afghans, as well as heavy construction equipment and engineers to help rebuild the country.

The poor security in Afghanistan still hinders reconstruction efforts. Many parts

Al-Qaeda Strikes Again

The victory over the Taliban in the fall of 2001 did not end terrorism in Afghanistan or elsewhere. The new government of Afghanistan, as well as U.S. troops and peacekeeping forces (the International Security Assistance Force) sent from Europe, provided a wealth of new targets for suicide bombings, which began in the days after the fall of Kabul.

In early June 2003 four German peacekeepers were killed when a taxi filled with high explosives detonated alongside their bus. The suicide bomber had ties to the Taliban as well as al-Qaeda. The goals of these groups, which no longer have conventional ground troops to fight with, are to destabilize the new government and make the occupation by foreign security forces unpopular in Europe and the United States.

of Afghanistan remain heavily damaged by the bombing and ground fighting of 2001. Minefields and unexploded bombs still threaten rural villagers. Militias opposed to the new government fire rockets and mortars into Kabul and against government targets in other cities. If the situation continues, the Afghans may turn their frustration and anger against the United States, and the Taliban, or organizations much like them, may return in force. There are thousands of men in Afghanistan still armed and ready to rejoin one of these factions should Afghanistan again descend into violence.

Ahmed Rashid and Barnett Rubin, in an opinion piece published in the *Wall Street Journal,* stated that "As long as [warlords] can threaten people, Afghans will not be free to debate and institutions will not be able to function. . . . People in Iraq and elsewhere are watching to see if the U.S. is committed not only to defeating regimes it sees as threats, but to providing security and governance to the long-suffering people of those countries. They will draw their conclusions according to the results."[14]

The Afghan campaign may serve as the model for future battles in the War on Terrorism. But the war in Afghanistan demonstrates that such battles may take years to conclude. The new Afghan government rules a disordered and violent country, one that still provides shelter for groups hostile to the United States. Providing an orderly transition to democracy in Afghanistan has proven to be a much tougher task than routing al-Qaeda and the Taliban.

★ Chapter 4 ★

Preemptive War: Iraq

After the war in Afghanistan the focus of the War on Terrorism shifted to Iraq. In the spring of 2003, the United States carried out a preemptive war against Iraq, which means that the United States attacked Iraq without an immediate threat or provocation. The United States claimed that it sought to end Iraqi support of terrorism and the threat of suspected Iraqi weapons of mass destruction. The war in Iraq was also aimed at destroying the Iraqi regime of President Saddam Hussein and installing a government friendly to the United States. The controversy surrounding the stated goals of the war, as well as the enormous challenges of keeping the peace, created problems for the United States in Iraq immediately after the end of the war, however. It remains to be seen whether the war in Iraq will be considered a success.

Justifying the War

The War on Terrorism was not the first time the United States and Iraq had clashed. The two had been to war a little more than a decade earlier, during the 1991 Persian Gulf War. At the end of that war, the United Nations passed economic sanctions that barred Iraq from normal trade but did allow it to sell crude oil in exchange for food and medicine. The UN also determined that Iraq could not be trusted with weapons and ordered it to destroy its chemical and biological weapons, destroy its long-range missiles, and end its nuclear weapons research. On their journeys within Iraq, the inspectors discovered stockpiles of several deadly chemical and biological agents, including anthrax, botulinum toxin, mustard gas, sarin, and VX nerve gas. In addition, defectors from Iraq told of a secret nuclear weapons program, in which Iraq was carrying out research into nuclear weapons at several different locations.

Although Iraq had suspended the weapons inspections in 1998, it allowed the inspectors to return after the terrorist attacks of September 11. The attacks swayed international opinion in support of the United States, and Iraq cooperated again in order to head off a confrontation. But the Bush administration claimed that Iraq was still in violation of the terms of the 1991 treaty. Bush announced that if Iraq did not cooperate with weapons inspectors and publicly destroy its weapons of mass destruction, the United States would take steps to bring the regime of Saddam Hussein to an end.

In late 2002, the Bush administration began a buildup of military forces in the Persian Gulf. In a speech to the United Nations given in February 2003, Secretary of State Colin Powell carefully laid out the case against Iraq. He claimed that the Iraqi regime continued to stockpile VX nerve gas and other chemical weapons, and accused it of continuing its nuclear research program. He also charged that Iraq had kept a secret arsenal of long-range Scud missiles, which were banned by the 1991 treaty. The United States also believed that Iraq was researching chemical and biological weapons in mobile laboratories. The laboratories were rumored to be in semitrailers that were being hauled by truck over the Iraqi countryside in an effort to conceal this research from UN weapons inspectors.

On several points, however, the United Nations disagreed with Powell and the United States. The weapons inspectors had verified that Iraq had destroyed its stockpiles of VX gas during the 1990s. The inspectors had also stated that there was no evidence of a revived program of nuclear weapons research. The UN inspectors had found no Scud missiles anywhere in Iraq; nor had they found stockpiles of chemical agents or chemical warheads.

Undeterred, the United States still sought justification to overthrow an unfriendly gov-

Iraqi president Saddam Hussein refused to comply with the terms of the 1991 weapons treaty on several occasions.

A line of U.S. armored vehicles arrives in Baghdad. Some members of the UN Security Council did not support the U.S. campaign against Iraq.

ernment on the grounds that one day Iraq might attack the United States. However, they had few tools left at their disposal. The economic sanctions had failed to bring down the Hussein regime. And although the United States supported opponents of Saddam Hussein within Iraq, these opponents could not manage a coup against their government. Many were captured, imprisoned, and executed, while many others fled the country. For Iraqis, speaking or acting in any way against Saddam Hussein, with or without the support of the United States, became too dangerous.

To achieve its goal the Bush administration decided to invade Iraq, destroy Hussein's regime, and politically transform the country. The U.S. military, it was hoped, would find and destroy the weapons of mass destruction that it believed Iraq was hiding and that the UN weapons inspectors had not found. The United States promised that after the war it would help establish a new Iraqi government and supervise elections for a new president and legislature. A democratic Iraq, Bush believed, might set an example for other nations in the Middle East.

Making the Case for War in the United Nations

The Bush administration did not want to fight Iraq alone, however. As in Afghanistan, it wanted to form a coalition to support the American military, lend diplomatic support, and help with humanitarian aid. So it turned to the United Nations in an appeal for support. Although Iraq had certified to the UN, in documents and speeches, that it had destroyed its arsenal, the United

States portrayed this assertion as a lie, and claimed that the use of military force was justified.

But many members of the UN, including NATO allies such as France, Belgium, the Netherlands, and Germany, resisted the use of military force. They stated that the United States was exaggerating the Iraqi threat in order to justify the war. They warned that the war might spread to neighboring nations and inspire terrorist acts against the United States as well as Europe. If Iraq did have weapons of mass destruction, these opponents stated, the inspectors should continue their job and keep up the pressure on the Hussein regime. In a full-scale war started by the United States, Iraq might use these weapons against the United States and Iraq's enemies in the Middle East.

The final decision rested with the fifteen nations that belonged to the UN Security Council, which has the authority to approve UN support for military action. In early 2003 the Security Council still did not support the use of force. In February, when the United States asked the Security Council for a final resolution authorizing force, most members of the council threatened to veto the resolution. The opposition to the resolution was led by France, Russia, and China, three countries that had formerly vowed to assist the United States in the War on Terrorism.

These allies in the War on Terrorism, particularly Western European allies, saw the United States as using the war against terrorism as an excuse to settle old scores against its enemies. They saw a threat of American imperialism and conquest as equally dangerous as the threat from small terrorist groups, who had left Europe in peace for many years. Although these nations had supported the war in Afghanistan, they wanted to resolve the conflict with Iraq peacefully. They announced that the inspectors should be given more time. As long as the United States and the United Nations threatened war against Iraq, they believed, Iraq would be unlikely to carry out any hostile actions against the United States.

While Great Britain remained supportive, the United States had to look for new allies in the fight against Iraq. American diplomats persuaded Spain, Bulgaria, Australia, Poland, and several other Eastern European nations to support the war. These nations pledged the use of small infantry and special forces units, reconnaissance planes, engineers, construction units, doctors, translators, and repair brigades. Many had their own particular motivations—for instance, closer ties to the United States and membership in NATO for nations such as Bulgaria. Out of these smaller and less conventional allies, the United States formed what it called the Coalition of the Willing. In the future, a changing "coalition of the willing" will likely become a normal facet of the War on Terrorism.

Fighting to Shock and Awe

Despite UN disapproval and mixed support at home, the United States decided to proceed without the support of the Security Council. On March 18 President Bush announced a final, forty-eight-hour deadline: Saddam Hussein had two days to comply with the UN's previous resolutions, destroy all of his weapons of mass destruction, and leave Iraq, or face a military offensive. When the deadline came and went with no action or announcement by Iraq, the war began on March 20.

The United States wanted a short war. If the Iraqi regime quickly surrendered or collapsed, military and civilian deaths would be minimal. A short war would also avoid extensive damage to Iraqi cities, oil fields, highways, and other infrastructure. This would make the reconstruction of Iraq after the war much easier.

To achieve a quick victory, the United States first attempted to kill Saddam Hussein. Satellite images fixed the coordinates of palaces and government buildings where Saddam lived and worked. These buildings were bombed and destroyed, but the strategy did not work. After the first few days of bombing, Hussein appeared on Iraqi television, walking in the streets of Baghdad, the Iraqi capital, and making speeches from an unknown location. Although the United States was destroying many important government buildings and military targets, Saddam appeared to have survived.

The war began, as in Afghanistan, with an aerial bombing campaign. Military planners called the bombing "shock and awe." The shock-and-awe strategy was described by U.S. Air Force colonel Gary L. Crowder as follows: "The effects that we are trying to create [will be] to make it so apparent and so very overwhelming at the very outset of potential military operations that the adversary quickly realizes that there is no real

Proclaiming the War Against America

Soon after the war in Iraq began, a top al-Qaeda leader, Ayman al-Zawahiri, urged Muslims everywhere to take up the fight against the United States. As quoted by Reuters journalist Miral Fahmy on May 21, 2003, al-Zawahri proclaimed,

> The crusaders and the Jews only understand the language of murder, bloodshed . . . and of the burning towers. . . . Carry arms against your enemies, the Americans and Jews. . . . Attack the missions of the United States, United Kingdom, Australia and Norway and their interests, companies, and employees. Turn the ground beneath their feet into an inferno and kick them out of your countries. . . . Do not allow (them) and other crusaders—the murderers of your Iraqi brothers—to live in your countries and enjoy their wealth and spread corruption.

Ayman al-Zawahiri (left) sits with Osama bin Laden during a 2002 televised speech.

alternative here other than to fight and die or to give up."[15]

The military continued with a campaign in which the prime objective was to sow confusion and miscommunication among the enemy. Heavy bombing disrupted communications, destroyed command and control centers, and leveled government ministries and Saddam's lavish palaces inside Baghdad. The goal, as in Afghanistan, was to minimize collateral damage and civilian casualties. The U.S. commanders believed that Saddam had little popular support within Iraq and that destroying key elements and symbols of the regime would bring about a swift collapse of the enemy's will to fight.

The Ground Campaign

It was hoped that this type of warfare would allow the United States to win quickly and decisively. But in the first week of the war, as two American infantry divisions invaded southern Iraq, the enemy struck back with small paramilitary groups. These units carried out hit-and-run attacks on U.S. troops and vehicles.

Terrorist tactics also slowed the advance. In the second week of the war, a suicide bomber blew himself up and killed four American soldiers at a checkpoint near the city of An Najaf, southeast of Baghdad. Iraq promised more such events and called on the rest of the Islamic world to rise up against the United States. To prevent an all-out terrorist campaign by the Iraqis, the United States asked many countries to expel Iraqi diplomats and intelligence officers from within their own countries on the grounds that they were a terrorist threat. This request, in nearly all cases, was refused.

After two weeks the American advance regained its momentum. U.S. troops advanced to the outskirts of Baghdad. Preparing for chemical warfare, American officers issued gas masks and protective clothing to U.S. troops in the field. They also planned for street fighting in Baghdad. This was expected to be the most difficult phase of the campaign. U.S. troops would fight for the streets and squares of Baghdad against entrenched Iraqi troops. The fighting was expected to be much more difficult than warfare in the open countryside.

The Fall of Baghdad

However, the expected urban warfare did not occur. U.S. troops entering Baghdad met little resistance. On April 9, in a central square of Baghdad, the fall of the regime was symbolized as Iraqi civilians began to gather and destroy a statue of Saddam Hussein. According to one eyewitness report from a CBS reporter, Lara Logan,

> It was really quite an emotional scene for many people watching here—especially for the Iraqi people to see American tanks on the streets of the capital. I think many people here never believed that this was possible—until they were seeing it with their own eyes.

A lot of people around me have disintegrated into tears as we watch this extraordinary scene unfolding below. People are being increasingly emotional and upset. Many people have said it's a violation of their nation's pride and dignity. This is something that the coalition forces are going to have to work very hard to overcome. Even those people who do not support the regime of Saddam Hussein still feel that in some way this is an occupation . . . one man said to me, "I may not like Saddam Hussein, but I don't like to see foreign invaders in my country."[16]

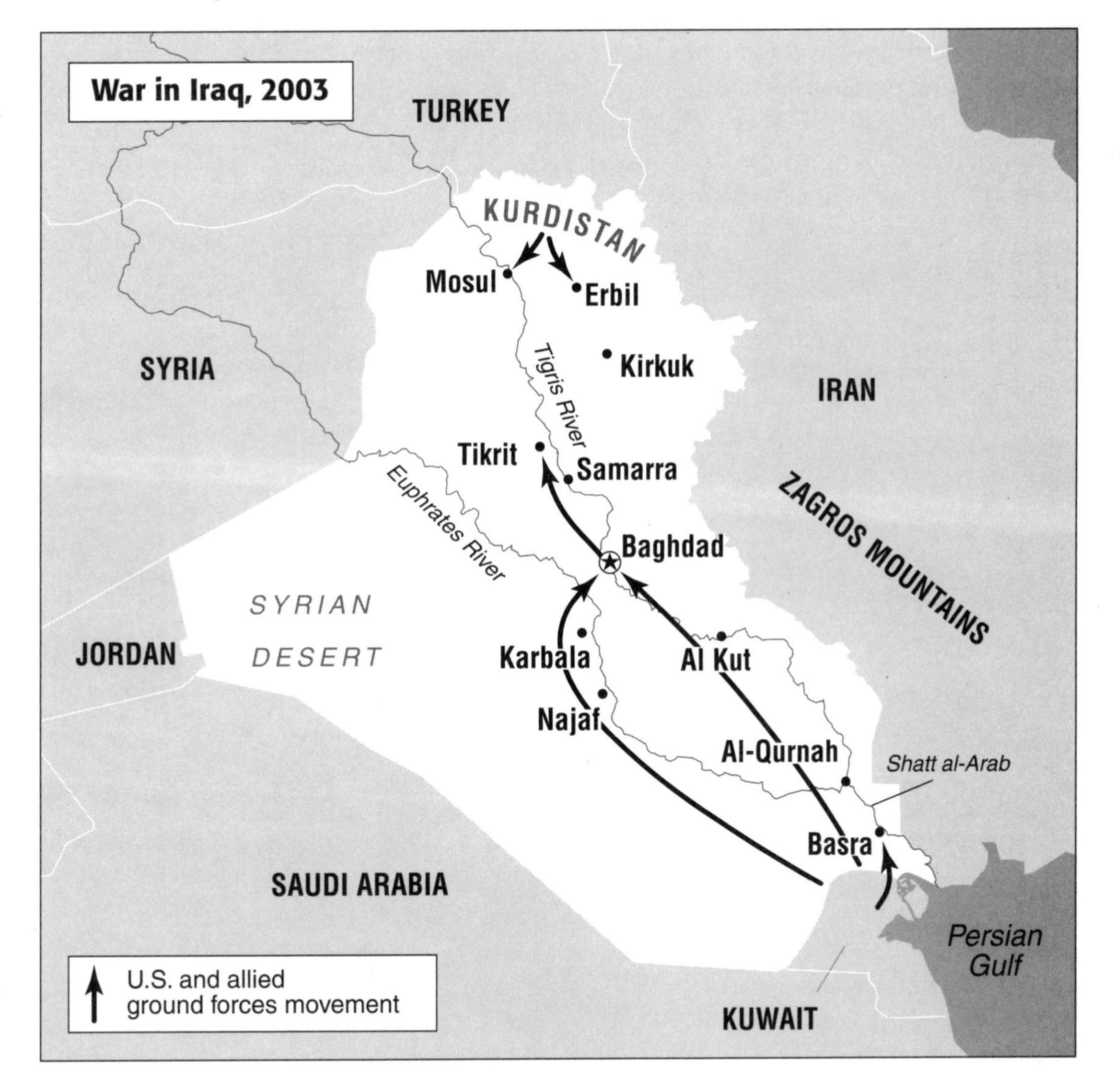

The fall of the Saddam Hussein regime took place in a matter of weeks. The military campaign had been a stunning and very swift victory for the United States. But violence in Iraq had not ended. After President Bush declared victory and an end to hostilities on May 1, attacks on U.S. and British forces continued. Guerrilla fighters loyal to Saddam Hussein continued to fight with sniper fire, rocket-propelled grenades, and car bombs. Hussein, himself, continued to elude capture, although his two sons—important symbols as heirs to his regime—were killed in a firefight in late July. By August, more than 120 American soldiers had been killed, and terrorist attacks against Iraqi civilians, against symbols of the U.S. occupation, and against U.S. allies took place on a weekly, if not daily, basis. Iraq remained a violent and unstable place, where creating an open and democratic government to replace the old regime grew into an incredibly complicated task.

Iraqi civilians in Baghdad throw stones at a burning picture of ousted president Saddam Hussein.

Rebuilding a Friendly Iraq

The second objective of the campaign in Iraq, to establish a friendly Iraqi government, will certainly take much longer than the military campaign and be much more difficult to achieve. When the regime of Saddam Hussein was toppled there was no government to replace it. Instead, the United States had to govern the country by occupying it and enforcing the occupation with a large number of troops. The United States also had to rebuild, from the ground up, a new police force, government ministries, and the Iraqi army. The power vacuum created by the destruction of Saddam Hussein's regime brought chaos and worsened the rivalries among Iraq's ethnic and religious factions.

In the meantime, Iraqi civilians suffered from the effects of the war. In the aftermath of the fighting, looters raided bank vaults, private homes, and the national archaeological museum. In many cities, there was no electricity for long periods of time. The war disrupted Iraqi oil production, the country's main source of income. Unemployment spread, and food remained scarce. Iraqi civilians grew angry and impatient with the lack of law and order in their towns, with the arrest and interrogation of civilians by U.S. troops, and with the continuing occupation.

To help the situation the United States repaired and restarted the Iraqi oil business. Money from oil exports was transferred into the Iraqi Assistance Account to pay for food, medicine, weapons inspections, repair of infrastructure, and setting up a new Iraqi government.

Searching for WMD

In the weeks before the attack on Iraq, the United States explained its reason for wanting war: Iraq's dangerous arsenal of chemical, biological, and possibly nuclear "weapons of mass destruction" (WMD). These weapons, it was claimed, could be used against Iraq's enemies in the Middle East, or sold to terrorist groups, who would then turn them on the United States.

However, despite extensive searches all over Iraq after the fall of Baghdad in early April 2003, no such weapons were immediately found. Many people questioned the information put forward by the CIA on Iraq's WMD, as it came to light that much of the intelligence used to justify the invasion had been incorrect or incomplete. The Bush administration was accused of playing up a false threat in order to justify a war. These accusations, and the controversy over whether the invasion was actually justified, will have long-term effects on U.S. strategy, both military and diplomatic, in the years to come.

The Elusive Smoking Guns

The search for Saddam Hussein's weapons of mass destruction continued, and largely failed. On May 9 members of the 101st Airborne found a mobile laboratory at the Al Kindi missile research and testing complex outside Mosul. Another such mobile lab was found April 19 near the northern Iraq town of Arbil. The Iraqis claimed the trailers were used to make hydrogen for weather balloons. Inspectors sent by the United States found no chemical or biological agents within the labs and eventually agreed with the Iraqis. In the meantime, seven nuclear weapons research sites were extensively damaged by looting that occurred after the fall of Baghdad. The looting resulted in the scattering of documents, equipment, and sources of radiation, while U.S. troops and civilian inspectors carried on a fruitless search.

The stated justification for the war on Iraq, that the Hussein regime was hiding weapons of mass destruction and threatening to use them against the United States, began to lose its credibility. The failure to turn up such weapons dealt a heavy blow to support for the war in the United States. It also created a political scandal in Britain, where Prime Minister Tony Blair had steadfastly supported the war and sent a large contingent of ground troops to help. As a result, the United States will not likely be able to count on future international support for large-scale military action against terrorist sponsor states that it cannot adequately prove are dangerous. The "coalition of the willing" may shrink, and the United States may find itself unable to call on allies—not even the British—in the War on Terrorism.

In the meantime, terrorism continued unabated within Iraq. Attacks against American and British forces took a daily toll; in early August, a car bombing took place in the center of Baghdad in front of the embassy of Jordan, a country that supported the war against Saddam Hussein. Nevertheless, Bush and his administration continued to justify the war, stating that an important state sponsor of terrorism in the Middle East had been eliminated, a country had been liberated from tyranny, and a democratic regime would be put in its place. The war in Iraq also served the U.S. government in an unstated manner: as a stern example to other nations in the region of the price of sponsoring terrorism against the United States. The violent aftermath, however, is setting a very different example for terrorists determined to undermine U.S. influence in the Middle East and elsewhere.

★ Chapter 5 ★

Military Cooperation: The Philippines

After September 11, the United States brought its War on Terrorism to the Southeast Asian nation of the Philippines. The United States offered to send troops and advisers to the Philippines to help that government fight terrorism in its own country. The purpose was to draw the Philippines into a closer military alliance with the United States, which would like to use the Philippine army and police as proxy forces that will fight on their own to fulfill American goals. Author James S. Robbins optimistically describes the means and the goals of the U.S. strategy in the Philippines:

> [The] purpose is to prevent the southern Philippines from becoming another staging area for international terror . . . the type of operation the United States will have to engage in to keep the terrorists on the run and prevent them from coalescing in new nerve centers to pursue their war against civilization. It promises to be a low-cost, low-casualty, high-impact operation of relatively brief duration.[17]

Not all Americans believe that military intervention will help the Philippines or the United States, however. If the United States becomes involved in a local conflict, it risks being perceived as a foreign invader that is meddling in local politics. The longer the U.S. military remains in the Philippines, therefore, the more it risks Filipino opposition. As popular opposition builds, support for terrorist violence against the United States may also grow.

Abu Sayyaf and Terrorism

The Philippines has been a scene of terrorism and political conflict for many years. Filipino Muslims living among a largely Catholic (95 percent) population are increasingly dissatisfied with life under a non-Muslim social and political structure. Muslims in the independence movement, Abu Sayyaf, have been ardently fighting to establish their own

Muslim-run territory on the large southern Philippine island of Mindanao, the home of many Abu Sayyaf leaders.

One of these leaders, Abdurajak Janjalani, was a Muslim cleric who fought alongside the Afghan mujahideen during the Soviet occupation of Afghanistan. At one point, Janjalani met Osama bin Laden, who was providing arms and money to the mujahideen. Bin Laden inspired Janjalani with the vision of a worldwide Islamic jihad, or struggle, against Western culture and institutions. As a Filipino, Janjalani was bitterly opposed to American influence in the Philippines. He saw the military alliance of the United States and the Philippines as a threat to his long-sought goal of a Muslim homeland on Mindanao.

When he returned home to the Philippines, Janjalani founded Abu Sayyaf (Arabic for "Father of the Sword"). Bin Laden helped provide the group with arms and money through his brother-in-law, Mohammed Khalifa, who lived in the Philippines. Another member of al-Qaeda, Ramzi Ahmed Yousef, shared information with Abu Sayyaf, and the two groups cooperated in terrorist incidents, such as the 1994 midair bombing of a Philippine Airlines jet flying from Manila to Tokyo, Japan. Yousef and Abu Sayyaf also planned but failed to assassinate Pope John Paul II during the pope's visit to Manila in 1995.

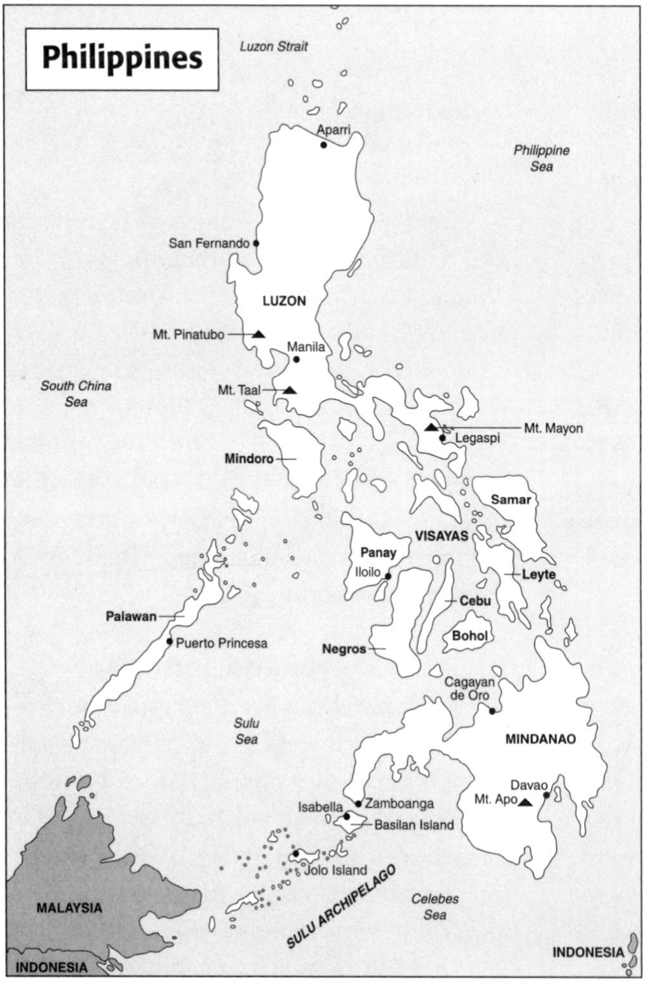

During the 1990s, Abu Sayyaf carried out several kidnappings, demanding ransom money in return for the safe return of their captives. The group took several hundred people hostage and murdered more than one hundred, usually by cutting off their heads. Their targets included tourists, missionaries, and wealthy Filipino citizens. The group also carried out bombings and at-

American missionaries are held captive for ransom by Abu Sayyaf guerrillas.

tacks on army posts and government buildings.

At the same time, the Muslim insurrection in Mindanao continued, with many battles settled by Abu Sayyaf and the Philippine military through an exchange of money or prisoners. Janjalani himself was killed in battle in 1998, after which Abu Sayyaf broke into two separate factions, one based on Basilan Island, the other on Jolo Island. The Basilan wing of Abu Sayyaf was one of many groups operating in the forests of western Mindanao and nearby islands when, in 2001, the Basilan group kidnapped three Americans and soon afterward beheaded one of their captives.

The geography of Mindanao and Basilan makes preventing such incidents nearly impossible. Long, winding coastlines allow small boats to carry guerrillas from one place to the next without being detected. The hills and forests provide plenty of hiding places and make control by a regular army extremely difficult. In addition, many local villagers are sympathetic to the Muslim insurrection and will not cooperate with the army of the Philippines. Several thousand Filipino troops are now hunting for a few dozen members of Abu Sayyaf, who can easily evade their enemies in the island's dense rain forests. As described by a *Time* magazine correspondent, "Stalking the rebels in jungle so dense that no light shines through the canopy of foliage, along jagged ridges often shrouded in fog, is like fighting in a dark closet with sunglasses on. The enemy are masters of the hit-and-run ambush, and might be lurking behind every curtain of vines, every thicket or frond."[18]

Rules of Engagement

The United States requested permission to send troops to the Philippines in January 2002, claiming it wanted to help the Filipino government destroy Abu Sayyaf once and for all and deprive al-Qaeda of an important partner group in Southeast Asia. President Bush worried that Abu Sayyaf might one day became as powerful as al-Qaeda, and take their fight outside of the Philippines to attack U.S. interests throughout the region.

The role of U.S. troops, however, is not a straightforward one and comes on the heels of a long and delicate military history between the United States the Philippines. In 1951 the two nations signed a mutual defense treaty, in which both countries pledged to help defend the other against any foreign aggression. The United States built and operated naval and air bases on Philippine territory. But in the mid-1970s, the people of the Philippines began calling for the U.S. military to withdraw from their country and close its bases. Many Filipinos saw the bases as small American colonies and claimed the United States was interfering in their government and trying to impose military control over them.

In 1991 the United States finally agreed to close down its bases in the Philippines, but in 1998 signed a Visiting Forces Agreement, which allowed the United States to still participate in military exercises of the Filipino army. U.S. troops may only take part in exercises designed to fight external aggression against the Phillippines and are not supposed to take part in any uprisings that take place within the Philippines.

The Visiting Forces Agreement is controversial because many Filipinos feel their army is simply being used to further American goals and that they are gaining little from the agreement. These opponents point out that the alliance has done little to curb terrorism in the Philippines. Instead, they believe, it has only caused further violence and political turmoil, as various factions in the Filipino government and military contest the issue of American intervention and military cooperation. In addition, they believe joint military exercises in the southern Philippines have inspired Abu Sayyaf and other groups to step up their efforts to create an independent enclave in this region.

It was in this atmosphere that the United States sent military advisers to the Philippines in 2002. A total of 660 U.S. personnel, including 160 members of special forces units such as Green Berets and Navy SEALs, took up their new bases in Mindanao and in Isabella, the capital of Basilan Island. Twelve-man teams were attached to Filipino infantry and marine units, teaching marksmanship, navigation, and the use of night-vision goggles and electronic surveillance equipment to help track Abu Sayyaf members through the rugged terrain.

The American troops had to adhere to predetermined rules of engagement to ensure that no treaties were breached during the mission. U.S. troops had to stay one thousand yards to the rear of any Filipino unit engaged in combat. They could not initiate combat, but were authorized to defend themselves should the need arise. In addition, according to the ground rules, the American troops remained under the orders of U.S. commanders and did not take orders from Filipino commanders.

The rules were designed to keep the U.S. troops out of the fighting. The Bush administration did not want American soldiers dying in the Philippines, which might sour the American public on involvement in the Philippines. The Filipino government also did not want the United States involved directly in the fighting, because it would make the Filipino army appear subordinate. Despite the efforts on both sides, the U.S. troops suffered casualties. The crash of a helicopter on February 22, 2002, killed ten U.S. troops, but there was little reaction in either the Philippines or the United States to this incident. Should American casualties continue, the Bush administration fears that the American public will begin to resist the deployment and call for it to end.

Controversy over the Deployment

Although there was little noticeable reaction to the soldiers' deaths, U.S. troop deployment has sparked a bitter political controversy in the Philippines. According to Article XVIII, Section 25 of the 1987 constitution of the Philippines, "foreign military bases, troops, or facilities shall not be allowed in the Philippines except under a treaty . . . ratified by a majority of the votes cast by the people in a national referendum [vote] held for that purpose."[19]

No such debate or vote was taken before the U.S. deployment of 2002, however, and many Filipino leaders sharply criticized the 2002 deployment as a violation of their constitution. Many of these critics asked why the supposed training exercises took place on Basilan, a combat zone. If the U.S. forces

A Raid in Manila

U.S. officials believe that terrorist groups can operate easily among the Muslim nations and neighborhoods of Southeast Asia. These areas provide havens for terrorist leaders, including important leaders of al-Qaeda, and can also provide recruits to their organizations. Strong evidence for this lies in a police raid that took place on a Manila apartment in 1995. The apartment was rented to Ramzi Ahmed Yousef, who was later convicted of planning the bombing of the World Trade Center in 1993. The police found plans to assassinate Pope John Paul II, as well as an elaborate plot to simultaneously destroy eleven U.S. passenger airplanes over the Pacific Ocean. Yousef is the nephew of Khalid Shaikh Mohammed, the mastermind of the September 11 attacks.

are only there to advise the local troops, many wonder why the excercises are taking place where the Muslim insurrection poses a much greater risk to the American troops than almost anywhere else in the country. Shariff Julabbi, a leader of the Moro Islamic Liberation Front, a group fighting in support of the Muslim insurgency, put it this way: "You do not hold war games in strife-torn areas . . . we are warning them not to encroach into our territories because we will surely respond drastically. . . . We will respond to any threats. We will shoot them if they encroach into our territories."[20]

In February 2003, the United States again proposed to send ground troops to the Philippines. This time, opposition within the country was even stronger. A bombing

at a Philippine airport in response to the plan persuaded the government of the Philippines to cancel it. The United States then proposed that the new "advisers" would only take part in training and investigation and would remain out of combat situations.

U.S. Marines arrive in Manila to help the Filipino government destroy Abu Sayyaf.

Opponents of the deployment accuse the United States of using the War on Terrorism as an excuse to return to the Philippines and establish a permanent military base in the country. Fear that this might happen has incited loud criticism of President Gloria Macapagal Arroyo, even among military officers. In July 2003, Arroyo's opponents in the military attempted a coup in Manila. The plotters had planned to ambush and kill the president and install a military junta, or ruling council. Although the coup was stopped, government investigators discovered in a search of computer files that more than three hundred officers were involved.

Arroyo has strongly defended her decision to allow U.S. troops into her country. The agreement with the United States has brought more than $100 million in military aid, Arroyo points out, as well as the promise of economic aid in the future. Quoted in the magazine *Frontline,* she stated: "Before making the decision to uphold the Balikatan (the joint U.S.-Philippine exercise), I was very much aware that it will be an issue that will be used against me, and that it entails some political risk. . . . I decided, however, to take the risk for the good of the country so the scourge of the Abu Sayyaf and other terrorists will be ended."[21]

Settling the Political Conflict in the Philippines

The United States has tried to alleviate tensions among the Filipinos by extending economic aid to the country as well. To win the support of the Filipino military, the United

The Jemaah Islamiya

The Philippines and several other Southeast Asian countries are home to a "regional" terrorist group known as the Jemaah Islamiya (JI). This group, led by a cleric named Abu Bakar Ba'asyir, fights to install a fundamentalist Islamic state across Southeast Asia. JI has operatives in Malaysia, Indonesia, Singapore, and the Philippines. The government of Australia has also accused the group of seeking to set up cells in northern Australia and of planning to annex this region to its future Islamic superstate.

Authorities in Indonesia believe that the JI was responsible for the bombing of a Bali nightclub on October 12, 2002, an attack that killed more than two hundred people. Eleven days after this attack, the JI was officially designated a terrorist organization by the Department of State. The group also planned an attack on the embassies of the United States and Israel in Singapore, but in December 2001 this plot was discovered and foiled.

The JI is also believed to be a close ally of al-Qaeda, which funnels money to the organization and uses it to carry out terrorist attacks in the region. Like al-Qaeda, the JI is organized into small cells, which operate independently of each other and take instruction from the group's top leaders.

Emergency workers on the Indonesian island of Bali remove a victim of a terrorist bombing of a nightclub.

States gave $100 million in military hardware to the army of the Philippines in 2001 and 2002. President Bush has also pledged $30 million of aid directly to Mindanao, the heartland of the Muslim insurgency. The money is to be used to improve public services, as scholarships for students in the region, and to support members of the insurgency who agree to lay down their arms and return to civilian life.

A permanent peace in the Philippines will be difficult to achieve, however. The poverty and isolation of many of the turbulent areas makes them breeding grounds for rebellion, violence, and terrorist attacks. The Philippines itself, according to an opinion written by Philip Bowring in the *International Herald Tribune,* may not be the best theater of operations for the War on Terrorism: "Mindanao's explosive mix of religious violence, civilian-military rivalry, smuggling and corruption makes it a poor base for closer American involvement in southeast Asia. The war on terror is better fought by cooperation with Muslim moderates and with democratic countries like Indonesia and Malaysia, which have sought to play a peacemaking role in Mindanao."[22]

The United States is also encouraged by many of its critics to address economic and social issues that cause dissatisfaction and desperation within foreign countries and prompt people to use terrorism. In "A 'Second Front' in the Philippines," author Walden Bello argues that the use of military force in the Philippines is misguided and will not solve global terrorism:

> For even if the Special Forces and their proteges [in the Philippine army] do decimate the Abu Sayyaf, the unchanged conditions of . . . discrimination, inequality and poverty will continue to breed extremist responses. Only an aggressive program of social and economic reform will break the cycle of injustice and terrorism. The Americans may leave after six months, but it will be the locals who will be left with managing a situation that is worse than before.[23]

This proxy style of warfare will always be controversial, both within the United States and in foreign countries where it takes place. Most nations do not want to see American troops on their soil in any capacity, because the presence of foreign troops and military equipment represents a loss of sovereignty over their own territory. Within the Philippines, the proxy war remains a source of bitter feuding that, in the summer of 2003, nearly brought about a military takeover of the government. It remains to be seen whether the American presence will make the Philippines safer from terrorism or have exactly the opposite effect.

Chapter 6

Buying an Ally: Pakistan

Pakistan lies on the front lines in the War on Terrorism. As a Muslim country and neighbor of Afghanistan, Pakistan was an immediate focus of the United States after the September 11 attacks. Pakistan's government, a military dictatorship ruled by General Pervez Musharraf, quickly agreed to help the United States. But many of its people opposed this alliance and demonstrated against the United States and Musharraf during the fighting in Afghanistan. Opposition parties in Pakistan have called for a violent revolution, and want to overthrow Musharraf to establish a fundamentalist Islamic government. These parties are supported by Pakistanis who are increasingly fed up with their country's economic problems and corruption.

Although the United States has given massive economic aid to Pakistan to bolster its police and intelligence services, the dollars flowing into Pakistan have given rise to corruption, bribery, and outright theft by government officials responsible for controlling and distributing the money. These problems make the alliance between the United States and Pakistan one of the most precarious in the War on Terrorism.

A Fundamentalist Homeland

Pakistan has long been a home of Islamic fundamentalism. During the 1980s Pakistan served as a haven and base for the mujahideen, the guerrillas who fought the occupation of Afghanistan by the Soviet Union. Many of the mujahideen were schooled in Pakistani *madrassas* (religious schools), where scholars and preachers railed against Western values and spoke out for fundamentalist Islam. The United States paid little heed to the religious beliefs of the mujahideen, as they were, for the moment, U.S. allies in the Cold War, which focused on countering Soviet influence around the world.

Members of the CIA regularly met with the mujahideen leaders in Pakistan to help plan the campaign against the Soviets in

Afghanistan. The American government sent money and weapons to Osama bin Laden and other mujahideen leaders. With the money, which was sent through Pakistani banks and by couriers, the mujahideen bought arms and ammunition, paid their fighters, and built training camps in Afghanistan.

After a long guerrilla war, the mujahideen finally drove the Soviets out of Afghanistan. Mujahideen leaders, including Osama bin Laden, then took up a new fight. They wanted the Islamic world completely purified of what they saw as corrupt Western culture. They wanted to banish American business and institutions from Muslim countries and to establish fundamentalist Islamic governments; they wanted Muslim societies to be regulated by a strict interpretation of the Koran, the Islamic holy book, and by Islamic law. Believing there should be no separation of religious and political life, they wanted Islamic religious leaders who agreed with their goals to be in charge. They saw an opportunity to fulfill this vision in the chaotic postwar environment in Afghanistan.

A civil war in Afghanistan ended with a new fundamentalist government, known as the Taliban, in power. Many of the mujahideen fought for the Taliban and were rewarded after its victory with important positions in the government. Believing that it could easily control its neighbor, the Musharraf regime in Pakistan allied itself with the Taliban and provided Afghanistan with military and financial support. Pakistani generals helped the Taliban fight their enemies within Afghanistan, and young men from Pakistani *madrassas* joined the Taliban armed forces. Many others joined the Taliban's close allies, al-Qaeda and Osama bin Laden, who used Afghanistan as a base for terrorist operations against the United States.

Making a Deal with Pakistan

Through the late 1990s, the United States paid little heed to Pakistan's alliance with the Taliban. The United States had been providing Pakistan with military and economic aid for decades and using Pakistan as a key ally against Soviet influence in South Asia. The American government was unlikely to pressure this key ally over its support of the Taliban. For the administration of George W. Bush, who took office in 2001,

Secularism Versus Fundamentalism

The two opposing strains of modern Islam—secularist and fundamentalist—are fighting an important battle within modern Pakistan. The Pakistani leader, General Pervez Musharraf, favors a secular Islam, one in which religious and civil functions remain separate. His model is the nation of Turkey, a Muslim nation with a strictly secular government.

Opposing secularism are fundamentalist religious leaders who believe that the tenets of Islam should determine the form of government and the legal system. Important models of such a state are Iran, Saudi Arabia, and the former Taliban government of Afghanistan. In these states, religious leaders hold much greater authority, and Islamic traditions influence the laws of the land.

fundamentalism in the remote, landlocked, and poor nation of Afghanistan was not a pressing issue.

After the terrorist attacks of September 11, however, the United States asked for Pakistan's help to topple the Taliban government. Pakistan has a long border with Afghanistan and, in a war against al-Qaeda and the Taliban, Pakistan could provide vital bases for American planes and troops to use. By using its own police and armed forces, the Pakistan government could crack down on Islamic fundamentalism, close the *madrassas,* stop bin Laden from recruiting al-Qaeda members in Pakistan, and curb the spread of fundamentalism to the rest of the Muslim world.

Pakistan was also asked to end diplomatic relations with the Taliban, to end shipments of fuel to Afghanistan, to prevent Pakistanis

Pakistani leader Pervez Musharraf (right) and Donald Rumsfeld talk with reporters during a 2002 press conference.

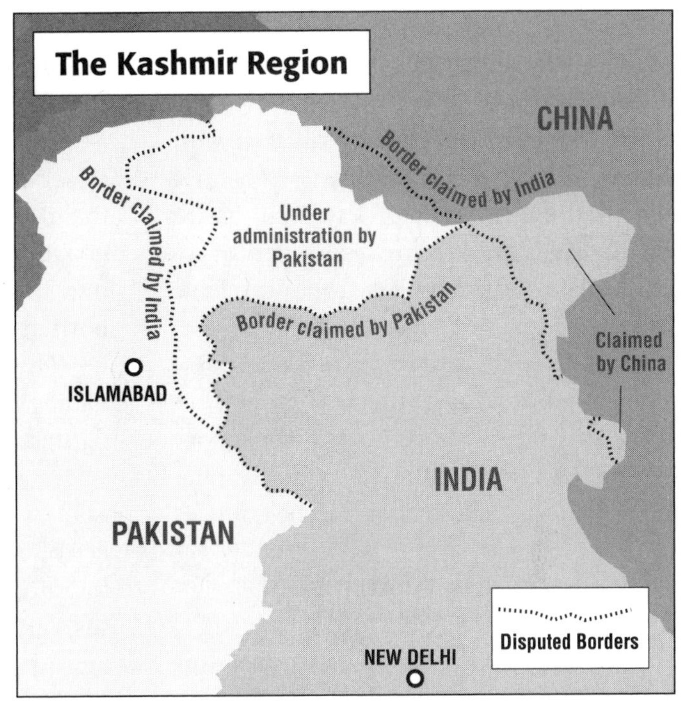

from joining the Taliban, to stop al-Qaeda members at its borders, and to intercept all arms shipments sent to al-Qaeda through Pakistan. The United States demanded the right to fly and land warplanes on Pakistani territory and the right to use naval and air bases in Pakistan. Pakistan was also asked for information about terrorist groups and individual members of al-Qaeda who lived in or traveled through Pakistan. In return for this cooperation the United States promised to extend loans and grants to help the country's struggling economy and provide weapons, planes, armored vehicles, and money to strengthen Pakistan's armed forces.

Musharraf had an important decision to make. If he agreed to help the United States, he risked anti-American turmoil in the streets of his country. Such chaos could weaken his regime or spark a revolution that would overthrow him. But he decided to cooperate, hoping that the military alliance with the United States would strengthen his government. Weapons and money from the United States would bolster the armed forces and help him to fight the fundamentalist opponents in his own country.

Musharraf was also attracted to the alliance because it put him in the position to befriend any new Afghan government that came to power after the Taliban. Pakistan has fought several wars with India, its more powerful neighbor to the east, and it does not want hostile governments on both of its borders. Musharraf also sought help from the United States with its relationship with India. The United States had threatened to brand Pakistan as a terrorist nation if it did not help fight the war on terror. If that happened, India would gain the upper hand, and the United States might support India's claims on Kashmir, a territory where Pakistan and India have been disputing their common border since 1947.

The alliance with the United States also put Pakistan in the position to improve its economy. Investment from the United States would help companies in Pakistan build new factories, make more goods, bring more foreign trade, and create new jobs for Pakistani workers. If the people of Pakistan saw their economy and living conditions improve, they might support the alliance with the United States. These factors clearly swayed the president of Pakistan, as he stated: "Pakistan is facing a very critical situation. The decision we take today can have far-reaching and wide-ranging consequences. The crises are too strong and too widespread. If we take the wrong decision in this crisis it can lead to even worse consequences. On the other hand, if we take the right decision, its results will be good."[24]

The War in Afghanistan and Its Aftermath

In September 2001 many U.S. officials worried how the Pakistani people would react to a war on the Taliban. For one thing, the Pakistani government had helped create the Taliban, and many Pakistanis worked for the Taliban either as soldiers or administrators. Secondly, many Pakistanis applauded the Taliban for installing an Islamic government in Afghanistan and bringing order to a chaotic land. Some Pakistani religious leaders promised a direct attack on the Musharraf government if Musharraf helped the United States. Although there were many street protests and some violence, the Pakistani army and police kept the situation under control. After the defeat of the Taliban, the streets of Pakistani cities calmed.

True to its word, the United States boosted its direct financial aid to the Pakistani government. Pakistan received more than $1 billion in aid in 2002 alone. At the same time, the CIA sent millions of dollars to the Pakistani intelligence service, known as the Interservice Intelligence Agency (ISI). Using the money to buy information from informers, the ISI then hunted down and arrested hundreds of suspected terrorists within its borders.

This cooperation also did permanent damage to al-Qaeda. Many fleeing al-Qaeda fighters and leaders took shelter within Pakistan, either along the border with Afghanistan or in Pakistani cities. The Pakistani police offered rewards in Pakistani newspapers for information on these suspects. Tips from suspicious neighbors led to the arrests of key al-Qaeda members, including Abu Zubaydah, the man who became al-Qaeda's military commander after the death in Afghanistan of Muhammad Atef.

The arrest of Zubaydah was an important victory in the War on Terrorism. Police searched Zubaydah's house after the raid and found notebooks, computers, records, and a satellite phone, which stores telephone numbers of those who send and receive calls. This information allowed the Pakistani police to track many suspected terrorists by using electronic listening devices provided by the FBI and the CIA. The capture of Abu Zubaydah also led to the capture of a Chicago man named Jose Podilla. The FBI believes that Podilla was working with al-Qaeda and was planning an attack inside the United States to release a radioactive "dirty bomb."

A Frontier Town and al-Qaeda

After the Afghan war, the United States and Pakistan continued to cooperate in the hunt for al-Qaeda members. Their efforts have concentrated on Pakistan's North-West Frontier Province. This region, which borders Afghanistan, is under only loose control of the central Pakistani government. Islamic fundamentalism thrives among the poor farmers and townspeople of the province. Refugee camps near the city of Peshawar, in particular, have provided good cover for al-Qaeda fighters escaping from U.S. troops in Afghanistan.

Al-Qaeda has a long history in Peshawar. This city was an important headquarters for the mujahideen—and for Osama bin Laden—who were fighting against the Soviet occupation of Afghanistan. Bin Laden himself recruited mujahideen fighters among the people of Peshawar and the surrounding countryside. In 1988 he came to this city to gather a small group of fighters and form al-Qaeda.

In September 2002, Zubaydah's arrest led to the capture of Ramzi Binalshibh, who coordinated payments to the nineteen hijackers who carried out the September 11 attacks. The most spectacular success occurred on March 1, 2003, with the capture of Khalid Shaikh Mohammed, the main organizer of the September 11 attacks. Mohammed was captured by the Pakistani police and turned over to the United States. His arrest had the effect of starting a long chain reaction in the investigation and arrest of al-Qaeda suspects, as detailed by journalist David E. Kaplan:

> Making the haul even better was [the arrest of Mohammed's] companion, Mustafa Ahmed al-Hawsawi. . . . With Hawsawi, agents found bank ledgers, the names of couriers and financiers, more phone numbers, and safe-house addresses. Investigators found an array of new suspects to track down, including more than a dozen sympathizers in America, Spain, and Switzerland. By spring of [2003], the Pakistanis were arresting al Qaeda suspects almost weekly.[25]

Continuing the search for al-Qaeda members, thousands of Pakistani soldiers patrolled the mountainous border with Afghanistan. The Pakistani police continued to monitor and infiltrate terrorist groups working within Pakistani cities. By the summer of 2003, Pakistan arrested more than four hundred suspected al-Qaeda members. The Pakistani government also froze the assets of several Islamic fundamentalist groups, banned their activities, and arrested their leaders.

At the prompting of the United States, Pakistan also cracked down on the *madrassas,* the religious schools that had educated so many al-Qaeda members. According to author Anatol Lieven, the crackdown includes

> imposing a broad, modern curriculum on the schools, registering all of their foreign students, and forcing them to cut their ties with militant training camps. [The United States] should keep the pressure on to ensure that [the Pakistani government] follows through on these efforts; the madrasas have become

training grounds for radical groups all over the Muslim world, and their graduates have caused mayhem in Pakistan itself as well as staffed the Taliban.[26]

Pakistan's Terrorism

Despite the help it has provided the United States in the war against terror, Pakistan is reported to practice terrorism to suit its own needs. Pakistan allegedly supports a militant Islamic movement that uses terrorist tactics in the disputed region of Kashmir to fight for a separate homeland for Muslims. In this struggle, Pakistan allows many groups labeled as terrorists by India as well as the United States to operate in the open, to clandestinely cross the border into India, to operate safe houses in Pakistani cities, and to run arms and money to Kashmir's Muslim militants.

Pakistan uses this Muslim separatist movement as a weapon in its own political battles with India. The Pakistani government believes the Kashmir militants are waging a legitimate political struggle, and so will not crack down on groups who commit violence on behalf of this struggle. Pakistan views the U.S.-led war against terrorism as an entirely separate issue. To keep Pakistan's cooperation, the United States mutes its criticism of the Muslim separatist movement in Kashmir and tries to carefully balance support for India and Pakistan in the dispute.

The Jaish-e-Mohammed

One of the most significant Islamist groups within Pakistan is the Jaish-e-Mohammed (JEM), or the Army of Mohammed. This group was formed in February 2000 by Maulana Masood Azhar. The goal of the JEM is to unite the disputed province of Kashmir with Pakistan, and bring Kashmir's Muslims under Pakistani rule.

The JEM has carried out a long campaign of bombings and assassinations, which India labels terrorism, in an attempt to destabilize Kashmir and instigate a civil war. The group was closely allied with the Taliban and Osama bin Laden, and received money and arms from al-Qaeda. The United States demands that Pakistan crack down on this group to demonstrate its willingness to help in the War on Terrorism, but the people of Muslim Pakistan support the group's goals in Kashmir. Arresting JEM leaders and attempting to destroy the group would be unpopular in Pakistan, which has had a long border conflict with India over Kashmir, so the Pakistani government allows the group to plan and carry out its operations. The definitions of "terrorism" and "war" are quite vague and changeable in South Asia.

Maulana Masood Azhar heads Pakistan's militant Jaish-e-Mohammed.

The United States hopes to prevent another war between India and Pakistan, which have fought over Kashmir three times since 1947. Such a war might disrupt the effort against al-Qaeda, or even bring the Musharraf government to a violent end should Pakistan lose. An India-Pakistan war might also turn into a nuclear confrontation, as both nations possess nuclear weapons.

Nuclear proliferation has become a pressing issue in the War on Terrorism. A future terrorist attack might be made not with airplanes or car bombs but with a nuclear device. There are very few sources of nuclear weapons, which are under tight controls in the countries where these exist. One of these countries, however, is Pakistan, a country with a history of political instability and an ongoing conflict with its neighbor. If the Pakistani government weakens, its military might be vulnerable to a raid or an attack on its nuclear facilities. If this happens, a nuclear weapon might fall into the wrong hands and have devastating consequences.

U.S. Goals in Pakistan

The United States wants to maintain a strong and stable Pakistani government, and will therefore continue its military and economic assistance to Pakistan. The United States hopes that economic help will ease the widespread poverty in Pakistan. If Pakistanis see their lives improving, they might turn away from the fundamentalist groups that call for a revolution, and which support al-Qaeda and other terrorist groups against the United States.

However, many Pakistanis see the United States, and not Osama bin Laden, as the real threat to their country's sovereignty. They believe America is simply buying the loyalty of their government, and they believe this brings further corruption to the military regime that rules their country. Although Pakistan has proven to be one of the most valuable allies in the War on Terrorism, its help and support might quickly disappear if President Musharraf finds himself out of power.

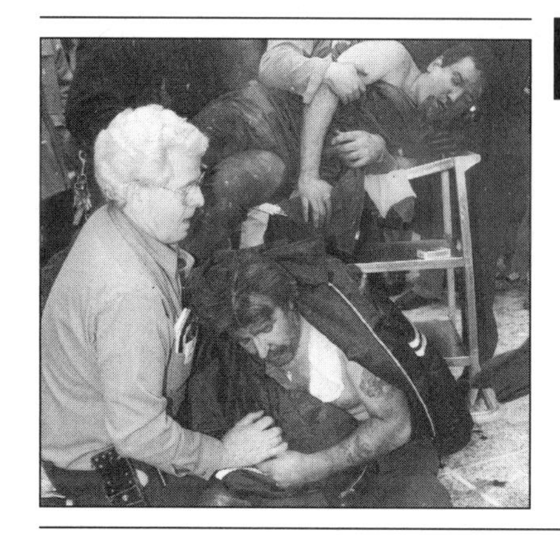

✯ Chapter 7 ✯

Saudi Arabia: An Elusive Ally

Saudi Arabia has long been a close ally of the United States, despite the fact that the two nations differ sharply in their politics and culture. Saudi Arabia is a monarchy, where a single family rules absolutely. Saudi Arabia, the birthplace of Islam, allows no other faith within its borders and has turned a strict form of Islam into a state-sponsored religion.

The Saudi-American relationship is based on Saudi Arabia's immense supply of oil. Home to one-fourth of the earth's known oil reserves, Saudi oil is essential to modern industrial economies. In turn, money from oil sales is essential to Saudi Arabia, which has few other natural resources. "Petrodollars," the money earned from oil sold for American dollars, flows into the treasury of the Saudi government and is then distributed directly to members of the Saudi royal family. This flow of money has brought corruption to the highest levels of Saudi society and breeds resentment among ordinary Saudi workers, many of whom live in poverty.

In addition to needing Saudi oil, the United States also needs access to its strategic location in the Persian Gulf. The U.S. government established bases in Saudi Arabia in 1991 in order to fight the Persian Gulf War against Iraq, which shares a long border with Saudi Arabia. The United States also used Saudi Arabian bases during the 2003 campaign against Iraq. Saudi Arabia is one of only a few Middle Eastern nations that will allow the Americans to use its territory in this way and thus is a valuable ally for the United States to have in that region.

Saudi Arabia, however, has a shadowy involvement with terrorism. Many of its wealthy citizens are suspected of making donations to al-Qaeda, and even some members of the royal family are thought to have both knowingly and unknowingly contributed to terrorist campaigns. This history of financial support within Saudi Arabia for terrorism makes U.S.-Saudi cooperation in the War on Terrorism difficult. Because the United States needs Saudi Arabia as an ally, and as a source of oil, it proceeds very cautiously in fighting the War on Terrorism on Saudi territory.

The American Military and Saudi Arabia

The Saudi ruling family has had a long and prosperous relationship with the United States. During World War II, President Franklin Roosevelt pledged to protect Saudi Arabia from its enemies in exchange for free access to Saudi oil. In 1971, to protect this oil supply and to bolster its most important ally in the troubled Middle East region, the United States deployed military advisers and weapons to Saudi Arabia. The United States also equipped and trained the Saudi Arabian National Guard (SANG), a force that dealt with internal opposition to the Saudi monarchy.

In 1979 the Soviet invasion of Afghanistan and the overthrow of the shah of Iran by Islamic revolutionaries inspired the "Carter Doctrine," formulated by the administration of President Jimmy Carter. The doctrine held that any hostile attempt to gain control of the Persian Gulf region would be resisted by any means necessary. The U.S. military deployed a force composed of ships, planes, armored vehicles, and infantry, to maintain a presence in the region. To further monitor the oil-rich region, the United States used military bases in Bahrain, Oman, Saudi Arabia, and on Diego Garcia, an island in the Indian Ocean.

In 1991 the American military protected the Saudis from an invasion of their northern neighbor, Iraq, during the first Gulf War. The U.S. administration persuaded Saudi Arabia to allow U.S. ground forces to use bases within Saudi Arabia. After the war, the United States continued to use these bases to patrol a "no-fly zone" in southern Iraq, where Iraqi planes were prevented from flying missions.

Bin Laden's Grievance Against Saudi Arabia

The rivalry of Osama bin Laden with his homeland of Saudi Arabia has roots that go back to the first Gulf War, when U.S. troops arrived to shield the kingdom and its oil resources from an expected attack from Iraq. Before about five hundred thousand American troops arrived, however, bin Laden offered to do the job himself, using a company of mujahideen fighters who had recently driven the Soviet Union out of Afghanistan. When the offer was rejected and the United States was allowed to station troops and aircraft in northern Saudi Arabia, bin Laden vowed to take up arms against both nations.

Bin Laden expresses his opposition in religious and cultural terms. But his true motivation, many believe, is political power and influence within Saudi Arabia. Standing in his way is the United States, as well as the powerful Saudi National Guard, a force of one hundred thousand troops that was set up to counter the Saudi regular army and prevent any coup attempt. The goal of bin Laden may be to win influence over the national guard. His organization may have begun to reach that goal, as national guard weapons have already been found in the hands of al-Qaeda terrorists within Saudi Arabia.

The Saudi alliance with the United States has earned the contempt of many Saudis. The most famous Saudi who disapproves of the U.S.-Saudi relationship is Osama bin Laden, who has expressed his opinion of the two nations in this way:

> Our main problem is the U.S. government. . . . By being loyal to the U.S. regime, the Saudi regime has committed an act against Islam. . . . We declared jihad [holy war] against the U.S. government because the U.S. government . . . has committed acts that are extremely unjust, hideous, and criminal. . . . This U.S. government abandoned humanitarian feelings by these hideous crimes. It transgressed all bounds and behaved in a way not witnessed before by any power in the world.[27]

Bin Laden and those who follow him believe that without the support of the United States, the Saudi monarchy would not survive. Only American military might, in their opinion, protects the Saudi king from his external and internal enemies.

U.S. Marines board helicopters during a 1991 deployment exercise in Saudi Arabia.

Thus they blame the United States for perpetuating the repression of the Saudi government, which prolongs the poverty and suffering of the people.

Saudi Corruption and the Growth of al-Qaeda

Many citizens of Saudi Arabia accuse the Saudi royal family, which lives off the country's oil wealth, of being corrupt. The members of the royal family live directly off government stipends. Many Saudi Arabian princes build lavish homes, where they live idly and produce nothing for the country. This lifestyle sharply contrasts with that of many hardworking but poor Saudi citizens.

The Saudi people have no way to protest this corruption. There is no legislature; there are no political parties or free speech rights. The regime outlaws all forms of political debate, and enforces their laws with arrests, torture, prison sentences, deportations, and executions. Resentment for the regime has allowed many underground opposition groups, like Osama bin Laden's group al-Qaeda, to flourish.

Osama bin Laden's ultimate objectives are to overthrow the Saudi monarchy and to expel Americans from the Middle East.

Fundamentalist Islam and Terrorism

Bin Laden has also focused on the Saudi-American relationship as a cause of suffering of Saudi citizens. He views Westerners, and particularly Americans, as unclean "infidels," or religious outsiders. These outsiders, in his view, should not set foot within the kingdom of Saudi Arabia, where the prophet Muhammad founded Islam in the early seventh century A.D. All Muslims—not just fundamentalists—consider Saudi Arabia, the birthplace of Muhammad and the place of important Islamic shrines, as the holiest land of Islam, but the overwhelming majority do not share bin Laden's views.

Bin Laden's ultimate objective, which he views as a religious obligation, is the overthrow of the Saudi regime and the banishment of U.S. forces and influence from the Middle East. Author Michael T. Klare, in his essay "The Geopolitics of War," explains as follows:

> Bin Laden himself . . . is most concerned about Saudi Arabia. Ever since the end of the [first] Gulf War, he has focused his efforts on achieving two overarching goals: the expulsion of the American "infidels" from Saudi Arabia (the heart of the Muslim holy land) and the overthrow of the current Saudi regime and its replacement with one more attuned to his fundamentalist Islamic beliefs. . . . It is this reality, more than any other, that explains the terrorist strikes on U.S. military personnel and facilities in the Middle East, and key symbols of American power in New York and Washington.[28]

Some Saudi citizens agree with these objectives, and want to see bin Laden's vision of an Islamic society installed throughout the Muslim world. To this end, certain Saudi individuals support Muslim charities and schools that preach the tenets of Wahhabism, a Muslim sect that originated in the eighteenth century and that preaches what it considers to be a "pure" form of Islamic worship. Wahhabism enforces strict Islamic customs and laws, and completely rejects foreign culture and influence in the Islamic world.

Wahhabi preachers dominate Saudi religious life, and their books and sermons emphasize that the presence of "infidels" (unbelievers in Islam) on Saudi soil is an insult to Allah. Many authors, including Dore Gold in the book *Hatred's Kingdom: How Saudi Arabia Supports the New Global Terrorism,* link modern terrorism to these teachings of Saudi Wahhabism: "The ideology of hatred underpinning the attacks of September 11, 2001, had roots that were more than 250 years old. . . . This ideology of hatred was a product of Saudi Wahhabis . . . and the Saudi regime has been a key backer of Wahhabism's international terror network."[29]

Bin Laden's Goals

Like many young men growing up in Saudi Arabia, bin Laden was steeped in Wahhabi fundamentalism. When bin Laden returned to his homeland after helping oust the Soviets from Afghanistan during the 1980s, he was enraged by the presence of American troops and bases on Saudi territory. Many people within Saudi Arabia agreed that the American presence was contrary to the tenets of Wahhabism. Writing in the summer of 2002, author Eric Rouleau commented:

> Despite official denials, the U.S. troops, who have been in Saudi Arabia ever since the Persian Gulf War, are highly unpopular. In keeping with strict government orders, the issue is not raised in the media or in public. In private, however, many Saudis complain that they consider it a form of occupation—at best humiliating, since the regime should not have to rely on foreign protection.[30]

Osama bin Laden Celebrates

In the days after the September 11 attacks, Osama bin Laden took an opportunity to praise the hijackers and proclaim a victory in his war on the United States. Sitting before a video camera and holding a microphone, bin Laden delivered a short speech. As quoted by Bill Sammon in his book *Fighting Back: The War on Terrorism—from Inside the Bush White House,* bin Laden cited the American occupation of Saudi Arabia as the reason for the attacks.

> The Arabian peninsula has never—since God made it flat, created its desert, and encircled it with seas—been stormed by any forces like the crusader armies now spreading in it like locusts, consuming its riches and destroying its plantations. The United States has been occupying the lands of Islam in the holiest of places, the Arabian peninsula, plundering its riches, dictating to its rulers, humiliating its people, terrorizing its neighbors, and turning its bases in the peninsula into a spearhead through which to fight the neighboring Muslim peoples.
>
> . . . Every Muslim must rise to defend his religion. The wind of faith is blowing, to remove evil from the peninsula of Muhammed. . . . As to America, I say to it and its people a few words: I swear to God that America will not live in peace before peace reigns in Palestine, and before all the army of infidels depart the land of Muhammed, peace be upon him.
>
> God is the greatest. And glory be to Islam.

After the Afghan campaign, bin Laden set himself a new goal: to eject the Americans from Saudi Arabia and establish fundamentalist governments throughout the Muslim world. To this end, al-Qaeda has recruited members in Egypt, Pakistan, Saudi Arabia, and among the Palestinians. Bin Laden has built training camps in the Middle East and Asia to train these volunteers in terrorist strategy and tactics.

Bin Laden also seeks to destroy the U.S. alliance with the Saudi government. He believes that terrorist attacks will discourage the United States and prompt it to end its support of the Saudi regime. The loss of support, bin Laden hopes, will encourage a revolution. He ultimately wants to establish a radical fundamentalist state, and banish Western influence from the kingdom once and for all.

To this end, al-Qaeda members carried out several attacks on U.S. installations within Saudi Arabia during the 1990s. The United States asked Saudi officials to investigate the attacks, but these investigations never made much progress. While the Saudi government promised to cooperate with the United States, Saudi police made very few arrests. Those who were arrested were executed before U.S. investigators could question them.

The attacks of September 11, 2001, greatly concentrated the interest of the United States on terrorism originating in Saudi Arabia. Investigators discovered that of the nineteen hijackers who had committed the attacks, fifteen were Saudi natives. The American government and news media also noticed the lack of sympathy within Saudi Arabia for the United States in the wake of the attacks. In many editorials and articles Saudi journalists criticized the United States for its support for Israel, and portrayed the hijackings as a just and understandable reaction to that support.

Indeed, after the attacks bin Laden was viewed as a champion by those who dislike the United States for its power and wealth. Rouleau observed that "even though his actions may be seen as contrary to the precepts of Islam, al Qaeda's founder is considered a hero [in Saudi Arabia] for having challenged the United States by striking two key symbols of its power: the World Trade Center and the Pentagon."[31]

A Difficult Search

Such support for bin Laden makes locating terrorists in Saudi Arabia a very difficult task because it can be difficult to tell friend from enemy. While some Saudis sympathize with and support terrorists, others cooperate with the United States. Complicating matters are people, especially those in positions of authority, who may try to do both at once.

For example, an October 2001 raid on a Saudi government–supported charity's office in Bosnia turned up some suspicious items. NATO investigators found detailed photos of U.S. embassies in Kenya and Tanzania that were bombed by al-Qaeda in 1998. The photos were taken both before and after the bombings, indicating whoever took the photos was trying to study how effective the blasts were. Similar photos were found of the World Trade Center, along with information on crop-dusting planes, which can be used to spray

The Original WTC Attack

An international symbol of American economic power, the World Trade Center in New York has been a target of foreign terrorists since the early 1990s. The first plot against this target was planned within the United States and attempted in 1993. A truck bomb exploded underneath one of the towers, but did not succeed in its objective, which is described by author Bruce Hoffman in his book *Inside Terrorism:*

> We have also seen that the intention of the bombers of the World Trade Center in 1993 is believed to have been to bring down one of the 110-storey twin towers on top of the other and to release into the damaged tower a toxic cloud of sodium cyanide that allegedly would have killed any survivors of the initial blast. According to the judge who presided over the bombers' trial, had they succeeded, the sodium cyanide in the bomb would have been "sucked into the north tower," thus killing everyone there.

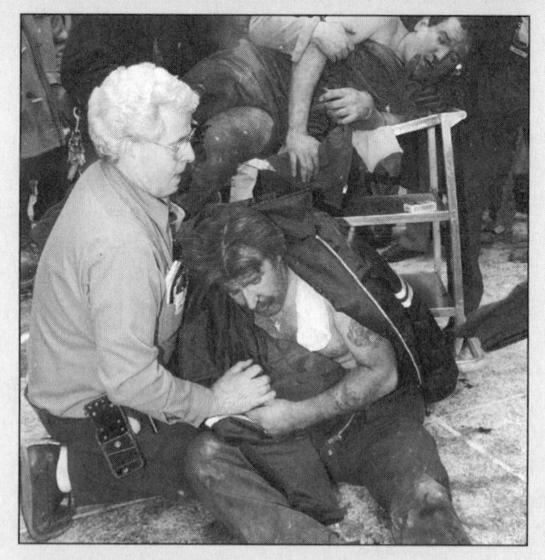

Rescue personnel aid victims of the 1993 terrorist bombing of the World Trade Center.

chemical or biological weapons over a wide area. These finds seemed to indicate Saudi support and potential involvement in these terrorist attacks.

On the other hand, Saudi officials have effectively helped fight the War on Terrorism. In November 2002, for example, Saudi police arrested Abd al-Rahim al-Nashiri, who is believed to have planned some of those same terrorist attacks. His arrest, along with similar moves to rein in terrorism, seems to indicate Saudi support for the United States. Such inconsistencies in Saudi policy make it unclear to what extent they can be counted as an ally of the United States.

Charity: Support for Terrorism?

Saudi Arabia is also an elusive ally when it comes to the matter of charity. It is no surprise that Saudi citizens support Islamic movements around the world with money they donate to private charities and religious foundations and schools. Americans also support their own religious institutions, charities, schools, and missionaries around the world. The difference is that supporting Islamic fundamentalists sometimes means supporting terrorism as a part of the religious work they do. For example, Saudi money that ends up in the hands of Hamas, designated by the United States as a terrorist organization, funds not only health, education, and welfare programs but terrorist attacks on Israel. In other situations, well-meaning Muslims are tricked into donating money to organizations that seem like legitimate charities, but are actually fronts for terrorist organizations.

Organizations such as Hamas used to keep separate accounts in Saudi banks to fund their terrorist activities, which usually require cash payments for arms, bombs, and other equipment. This practice has become more difficult, however. The Saudi regime, reacting to the alarm and criticism that this connection of charity to terrorism caused in the United States and elsewhere, passed new banking restrictions in June 2003. Charitable organizations must now be licensed by the Saudi government, may keep only one account, must verify their identity, and may make no cash withdrawals. With these new regulations, the Saudi government hopes to show that it is trying to prevent funds meant for charitable purposes from being diverted to terrorists.

An Attack in Riyadh

The importance of cooperating in the War on Terrorism became exceedingly clear to Saudis on May 13, 2003, when three car bombs went off in Riyadh, the capital. The bombs devastated three housing complexes, places where many foreigners—but also Saudi citizens—lived. The suicide attacks killed thirty-four people, including eight Americans. Saudi police arrested four individuals in connection with the bombings and linked those people to al-Qaeda, which had previously avoided such large-scale attacks in Osama bin Laden's homeland. Despite police and military efforts, it

The May 2003 suicide attacks in Riyadh left thirty-four people dead, including eight Americans.

was evident that the organization still had many adherents within Saudi Arabia.

The Riyadh attacks may prove to be a turning point in the War on Terrorism, as Saudi Arabia has now experienced terrorism against its own citizens. The Saudi government has promised to cooperate more closely with the FBI in terrorist investigations and to crack down on financing for al-Qaeda and other terrorist groups from Saudi individuals and organizations. Journalist Fareed Zakaria observed,

> For decades now, supporting Islamic extremism has been cost-free for the Saudis—government and people alike. They could appease militants, appear pious and buy themselves peace, all with little consequence. But now that Al Qaeda has for the first time killed Saudi civilians, the terrorist group might—just might—have destroyed the true basis of

its support. Fundamentalist terror is finally going to be fought in the Arabian heartland, the only place where it can be rooted out.[32]

The U.S. government wants to encourage the Saudi government to fight against terrorism. The United States is also pushing for more open political debate in Saudi Arabia, in order to lessen opposition to the regime. In the words of author Michael T. Klare,

When conditions permit . . . a serious review of U.S. policy in the Persian Gulf will be in order. Among the many questions that might legitimately be asked at this point is whether long-term U.S. interests would not best be served by encouraging the democratization of Saudi Arabia. Surely, if more Saudi citizens are permitted to participate in open political dialogue, fewer will be attracted to the violent, anti-American dogma of Osama bin Laden.[33]

☆ Chapter 8 ☆

A Staging Ground: Europe

Europeans have long been victims of political terrorism. Russian anarchists of the nineteenth century threw bombs and assassinated high officials to overthrow the czar (emperor) and his monarchy. In the early twentieth century, Serbian terrorists touched off World War I with violent acts against their Austrian overlords. During the 1970s small leftist groups in Italy, France, and Germany carried out random acts of violence to shake up the established order. Separatist groups are active in the United Kingdom and Spain. In various parts of Europe, politicians have been targeted for killing or kidnapping, military installations have been bombed, and ships and airplanes have been hijacked.

In addition to experiencing terrorism firsthand, Europe is commonly used as a staging ground where terrorists plot attacks that are carried out around the world. Europe makes an ideal staging ground because it is a patchwork of diverse states, languages, laws, and customs. These states do not act in unison, which can make it difficult to track terrorist movement across borders. Their courts uphold different laws and their police forces do not act in concert, making it easier for terrorists to evade law enforcement. Also, the borders of many European countries are porous; the European Union (EU), which includes most of Western Europe, allows free movement between its member countries. Terrorists often take advantage of this atmosphere to plan terrorist attacks to be carried out in other places. For example, several of the September 11 hijackers were significantly aided by an al-Qaeda cell that was active in Hamburg, Germany.

"Fertile Soil"

While the governments of European countries do not support terrorism, they have a difficult time reining it in. Many European countries lack the power to block the assets of known terrorist groups or their front organizations—groups that provide a false cover for running arms and explosives, or for diverting money to terrorist groups. Countries like Switzerland and Luxembourg have strict privacy laws regarding bank accounts. In those places it is illegal for a government or police force to demand access to banking records of a company or an individual. Therefore, Europe has not made the same progress as the United States in freezing terrorists' assets or following money trails to suspects.

Many European countries, especially France, Germany, and Great Britain, have large Muslim populations, and these governments proceed cautiously when arresting terrorist suspects or passing new terrorism laws. They fear that drastic restrictions might inflame Muslim immigrants to acts of violence. According to Jonathan Stevenson, "[European] Muslims . . . are only half-accepted socially and are politically

A Hamburg court sentenced this Moroccan man to fifteen years in prison for assisting al-Qaeda.

underrepresented. This marginal status makes them susceptible to radicalization—one factor that has helped prevent governments from taking steps that might seem anti-Muslim."[34]

Europe's method in the past has been to negotiate with terrorists in order to avoid violence. They have exchanged hostages, freed political prisoners, and released captured terrorists from prison. According to Stevenson, "This strategy [of negotiating with terrorists] allowed these groups . . . to preserve a place at the negotiating table even while they set off the occasional bomb."[35]

Europe is also an ideal staging ground for terrorism because its understanding of what constitutes terrorism differs from that of the United States. While the United States sees groups like Hamas, Hizballah, and the Philippine group Abu Sayyaf as terrorist groups, many Europeans support the independence causes of these groups and so label them as political parties that use violence for a legitimate cause. For this reason, many European states have not included such groups on their lists of terrorist organizations. According to author Roland Jacquard, the tolerance of political activity by terrorist groups has led Europe to become a hot spot of "Islamist" activity, much of it directly allied with al-Qaeda:

> In Belgium, with a population of more than three hundred thousand Muslims . . . radical Islam is primarily represented by the Muslim Brotherhood. . . . In Sweden, the Iranians and their armed wing Hezbollah dominate the scene. . . . Holland, with a community of four hundred thousand Muslims, including a wave of recent immigrants . . . has in the last few years begun to be an area of concern. . . . The Bin Laden Brotherhood thus had fertile soil in Europe.[36]

As a result of such an atmosphere, many of these groups have been able to recruit new members among European Muslim workers and immigrants, and they have been able to raise money in Europe to be sent to operatives in foreign countries.

The Aftermath of the September 11 Attacks

The September 11 attacks inspired widespread sympathy for the United States in Europe. In Paris, London, and other capitals, people marched to show support for the United States. European governments pledged help to the United States in its fight against al-Qaeda. They promised to cooperate with the FBI and the CIA to find and capture terrorists hiding in Europe. Many countries tightened their borders and established a database of fingerprints for those seeking asylum in Europe. European countries froze more than $30 million in suspected assets of al-Qaeda members and their cover organizations after September 11.

In addition, the members of the European Union created a new arrest warrant that helps the police forces of different countries work together. The warrant allows

The Missions of al-Qaeda

Al-Qaeda's operatives work and live in what are known as "sleeper cells," some of which are based in Europe. They remain in place, doing their best to blend into their surroundings, until called on to carry out an operation. Their loyalty is assured with constant contact with handlers, operatives who are responsible for training them and teaching al-Qaeda's principles and philosophy.

The following instructions are part of an al-Qaeda training manual found in the home of a member of the organization by police in Manchester, England. The manual is published on the U.S. Department of Justice website, www.usdoj.gov.

> The main mission for which the Military Organization is responsible is:
>
> The overthrow of the godless regimes and their replacement with an Islamic regime. Other missions consist of the following:
>
> 1. Gathering information about the enemy, the land, the installations, and the neighbors.
> 2. Kidnapping enemy personnel, documents, secrets, and arms.
> 3. Assassinating enemy personnel as well as foreign tourists.
> 4. Freeing the brothers who are captured by the enemy.
> 5. Spreading rumors and writing statements that instigate people against the enemy.
> 6. Blasting and destroying the places of amusement, immorality, and sin; not a vital target.
> 7. Blasting and destroying the embassies and attacking vital economic centers.
> 8. Blasting and destroying bridges leading into and out of the cities.

member countries to demand the deportation of suspected terrorists from other countries for one of thirty-two specified criminal acts. If, for example, Spain seeks to capture a terrorist who is known to be living in Holland, it can demand that local police arrest that suspect. The warrant bypasses long, complicated extradition hearings, which in the past had hurt the effort against terrorism on European soil. The arrest warrant was first used on January 16, 2002, when police arrested Juan Ramon Rodriguez in Amsterdam, a large city in the Netherlands. Rodriguez was wanted for conspiracy to murder on behalf of ETA, a group that seeks to establish a homeland for the Basque-speaking people of northern Spain and southwestern France.

Fighting the United States over Attacking Iraq

The unity enjoyed between Europe and the United States after the September 11 attacks was short-lived, however. When America's War on Terrorism came to Iraq, Europe and the United States were deeply divided on how to proceed. While the American government largely pushed for war, many governments and citizens in Europe favored increased sanctions and a diplomatic resolution to the problem. Many European governments trusted the United Nations to be the final arbiter of the conflict, and hoped it would be able to effectively prevent war.

The governments of Germany, France, and Russia especially opposed U.S. military

Demonstrators in Marseille, France, march to protest the U.S.-led war in Iraq.

intentions toward Iraq. (Great Britain, Spain, and several central European countries, however, supported the American stance.) Millions of people in these countries, and in the United States, took to the streets to protest a war against Saddam Hussein. Claiming it was a crucial undertaking in the struggle against global terrorism, in March 2003 President Bush decided that the United States would pursue military action in Iraq, even without the support of its traditional allies and the consent of the United Nations. From random allies and minor military powers, Bush collected a "coalition of the willing," whose members supported the U.S.-led invasion and conquest of Iraq.

Although the Iraq war attained the U.S. goal of ejecting Saddam Hussein from power, it left soured relations between the United States and several of its key European allies. In American newspapers, France was accused of supporting Saddam Hussein and resented for its unwillingness to take part in the coalition. France was denounced in the U.S. Congress, and many politicians called for a boycott of French products in the United States. For a short time, Americans even renamed French fries "Freedom Fries" to show their disdain for France's dissent.

France, in turn, was adamantly against the U.S.-led war in Iraq. France loudly argued that war was unnecessary and that Iraq did not harbor the weapons of mass destruction the Bush administration claimed it did. France and many other European countries lamented that the war caused hardship and misery in Iraq. They then claimed the war in Iraq has not prevented any terrorism, as Iraq was more volatile and chaotic after the war than it was before.

An Uncertain Path

The end of the war did not repair relations between Europe and the United States. France, in particular, remains a very uncertain ally, opposing many of the Bush administration's policies in postwar Iraq. While France wants the United Nations to take an active part in rebuilding Iraq, the United States resists this—it does not trust the United Nations to fulfill American goals there. European nations and the United States also disagree on the need for further weapons inspections, and what form a postwar government in Iraq should take.

These disagreements do not bode well for the fight against terrorism in Europe. Writing in September 2002, well before the outbreak of the war in Iraq, General Wesley Clark argued that European cooperation with the United States was already weakening:

> Last fall, all of Europe understood that the attacks of September 11 had been

A Fundamental Disagreement

Writing in the *Boston Globe* on June 5, 2003, editorialist Jeff Jacoby commented on the fundamental disagreement between Europe and the United States over the nature and the need for war:

> The truth is, Europe has lost its will to fight. The bloodshed of two world wars understandably left painful emotional scars and gave rise to a conviction—not so understandable—that war is fundamentally illegitimate and unjust. During the long Cold War, Western Europeans convinced themselves that the path to security lay in treaties, international bodies, and the downplaying of sovereignty—not in self-reliance and the projection of power. Safe and comfortable under America's military umbrella, they got used to the idea of having their freedom without having to defend it, or pay for its defense. Many Europeans came to see weakness and irresolution as virtues, embracing appeasement as the best response to aggression—and despising those who believe in peace through strength.

planned on European soil, that European targets were on the terrorists' lists, and that Europeans by the hundreds died in the World Trade Center. . . . Today, that support is being replaced by growing popular anger at the United States. Instead of focusing on the threat of terrorism, Europeans are focusing on the dangers of American hegemony [influence and power].[37]

Europe, as a result, may remain a haven for terrorists, a staging ground for terrorist attacks, and a convenient pipeline for the money, arms, and passports terrorists need to carry out their missions. If the United States wants to fight an effective war on terrorism in Europe, it will have to improve its relations with European governments and find a way to justify its policies and its methods to the European public.

★ Epilogue ★

An Ongoing War

The attacks of September 11, 2001, united the country with a common objective: the destruction of al-Qaeda. Since that time, the United States has mobilized itself against terrorism as never before. It has fought against the Taliban in Afghanistan and against the regime of Saddam Hussein in Iraq. Many of al-Qaeda's leaders have been killed or captured, and a very significant part of the organization has been disrupted. Journalist David E. Kaplan describes the situation as follows:

> Al Qaeda's wounds run deep. Over half of its key operational leaders are out of action. . . . Its top leaders are increasingly isolated and on the run. Al Qaeda's Afghan sanctuary [that is, its bases in Afghanistan] is largely gone. Its military commander is dead. Its chief of operations sits in prison, as do some 3,000 associates around the world. In the field, every attempt at communication now puts operatives at risk. The organization's once bountiful finances, meanwhile, have become precarious.[38]

Despite these achievements, al-Qaeda continues to recruit new members and plan terrorist strikes in foreign countries and within the United States. Though damaged, the group did survive the attack on Afghanistan, with many of its leaders fleeing to Pakistan, and adapted its methods to its new conditions. Rohan Gunaratna, author of *Inside Al Qaeda: Global Network of Terror*, describes the new targets and methods: "Al Qaeda has called for a change in modus operandi [working method] and choice of targets against the superior coalition forces [which fought against them in Afghanistan]. . . . Al Qaeda has also instigated Islamist terrorist groups to strike at foreign targets on their own soil as well as overseas."[39]

The war will continue for many years, perhaps decades. The only sign of success in the war will be a lack of new terrorist attacks, both in the United States and

Despite the fact that many members of al-Qaeda and the Taliban have been captured, the War on Terrorism continues.

around the world. Although the United States has not seen a major terrorist incident on its soil since September 11, there have been many such attacks in the Middle East and in Southeast Asia.

To declare victory in this war may never be possible. Terrorism has been used for many years and will continue to provide a useful weapon for those seeking to draw attention to a political cause. It can be seen as a kind of modern disease, one which thrives on mass communication and which can never be wiped out completely.

To succeed in this war, many believe that the United States cannot go it alone, and that U.S. officials must continue to muster support from other countries around the world. General Wesley Clark, a retired commander of NATO, expresses his opinion this way: "The longer this war goes on—and by all accounts, it will go on for years—the more our success will depend on the willing cooperation and active participation of our allies to root out terrorist cells in Europe and Asia, to cut off funding and support of terrorists and to deal with . . . other threats. We are far more likely to gain the support we need by working through international institutions than outside of them."[40]

Whether terrorism is best portrayed as a criminal phenomenon, a military problem, or a social challenge, it will likely continue to inspire new military strategies and involve the armed forces of the United States for a long time to come.

☆ Notes ☆

Introduction: A New Kind of War

1. Michael A. Ledeen, *The War Against the Terror Masters: Why It Happened. Where We Are Now. How We'll Win.* New York: St. Martin's, 2002, pp. xvi–xvii.

Chapter 1: Counterterrorism Abroad

2. Bill Gertz, *Breakdown: The Failure of American Intelligence to Defeat Global Terror.* New York: Penguin, 2002, pp. 10–11.
3. Roland Jacquard, *In the Name of Osama Bin Laden: Global Terrorism and the Bin Laden Brotherhood.* Durham, NC: Duke University Press, 2002, p. 90.
4. Anthony Lake, *Six Nightmares: Real Threats in a Dangerous World and How America Can Meet Them.* Boston: Little, Brown, 2000, p. 104.
5. Stephen Biddle, "Afghanistan and the Future of Warfare," *Foreign Affairs,* March/April 2003, p. 31.
6. Quoted in Kurt M. Campbell and Michele A. Flournoy, *To Prevail: An American Strategy for the Campaign Against Terrorism.* Washington, DC: Center for Strategic and International Studies, 2001, p. 371.

Chapter 2: Targeting Sponsor States

7. CNN.com, "Transcript of President Bush's Address," September 21, 2001. www.cnn.com.
8. Office of the Coordinator for Counterterrorism, "Patterns of Global Terrorism," U.S. Department of State, August 20, 2003. www.state.gov.
9. John Pynchon Holmes, *Terrorism: Today's Biggest Threat to Freedom.* New York: Pinnacle, 2001, p. 215.
10. Quoted in CNN.com, "Qaddafi: 'Libya Is Against Terrorism,'" July 11, 2002. www.cnn.com.

Chapter 3: Providing a Model: Afghanistan

11. Peter L. Bergen, *Holy War, Inc.: Inside the Secret World of Osama bin Laden.* New York: Free Press, 2001, p. 61.
12. Jamie McIntyre, "U.S. Propaganda to Taliban: 'You Are Condemned,'" CNN.com, October 18, 2001. www.cnn.com.
13. David E. Kaplan, "Taking Offense: The Inside Story of How U.S. Terrorist Hunters Are Going After al Qaeda," *U.S. News & World Report,* June 2, 2003, p. 21.
14. Ahmed Rashid and Barnett Rubin, "S.O.S. from Afghanistan," *Wall Street Journal,* May 29, 2003, p. A22.

Chapter 4: Preemptive War: Iraq

15. Quoted in Fred Kaplan, "The Flaw in Shock and Awe," Slate.com, March 26, 2003. http://slate.msn.com.

16. Lara Logan, "On the Scene: The Fall of Baghdad," CBSNews.com, April 9, 2003. www.cbsnews.com.

Chapter 5: Military Cooperation: The Philippines

17. James S. Robbins, "Freedom Eagle: The Mission in the Philippines," *National Review,* January 18, 2002. www.nationalreview.com.
18. Johanna McGeary, "Next Stop Mindanao," *Time,* January 28, 2002, p. 36.
19. About the Philippines, "The 1987 Constitution of the Republic of the Philippines: Article XVIII," August 20, 2003. www.gov.ph.
20. Quoted in Amit Baruah, "An Exercise in Intervention," *Frontline,* August 20, 2003. www.frontlineonnet.com.
21. Quoted in Baruah, "An Exercise in Intervention."
22. Philip Bowring, "Manila Can't Depend upon an American Crutch," *International Herald Tribune,* May 19, 2003. www.iht.com.
23. Walden Bello, "A 'Second Front' in the Philippines," *Nation,* March 18, 2002, p. 21.

Chapter 6: Buying an Ally: Pakistan

24. Quoted in Campbell and Flournoy, *To Prevail,* p. 188.
25. David E. Kaplan, "Taking Offense," p. 28.
26. Anatol Lieven, "The Pressures on Pakistan," *Foreign Affairs,* January/February 2001, p. 110.

Chapter 7: Saudi Arabia: An Elusive Ally

27. Bergen, *Holy War, Inc.,* p. 19.
28. Michael T. Klare, "The Geopolitics of War," in *A Just Response:* The Nation *on Terrorism, Democracy, and September 11, 2001,* eds. Katrina Vanden Heuvel and Jonathan Schell. New York: Thunder's Mouth, 2002, p. 275.
29. Dore Gold, *Hatred's Kingdom: How Saudi Arabia Supports the New Global Terrorism.* Washington, DC: Regnery, 2003, pp. 214–15.
30. Eric Rouleau, "Trouble in the Kingdom," *Foreign Affairs,* July/August 2002, p. 77.
31. Rouleau, "Trouble in the Kingdom," p. 78.
32. Fareed Zakaria, "Now Saudis See the Enemy," *Newsweek,* May 26, 2003.
33. Klare, "The Geopolitics of War," p. 276.

Chapter 8: A Staging Ground: Europe

34. Jonathan Stevenson, "How Europe and America Defend Themselves," *Foreign Affairs,* March/April 2003, pp. 76–77.
35. Stevenson, "How Europe and America Defend Themselves," p. 82.
36. Jacquard, *In the Name of Osama Bin Laden,* pp. 114–16.
37. Wesley Clark, "An Army of One?" *Washington Monthly,* September 2002, pp. 19–23.

Epilogue: An Ongoing War

38. David E. Kaplan, "Taking Offense," p. 20.
39. Rohan Gunaratna, *Inside Al Qaeda: Global Network of Terror.* New York: Berkeley, 2002, p. 299.
40. Clark, "An Army of One?" pp. 19–23.

✯ Chronology of Events ✯

1998

August 7: Bombs demolish U.S. embassies in Nairobi, Kenya, and Dar es Salaam, Tanzania; according to investigators, the bombings are planned and carried out by al-Qaeda.

2000

October 12: The U.S. Navy destroyer *Cole* is heavily damaged in the port of Aden, Yemen, when a small boat carrying explosives detonates while floating alongside; seventeen U.S. sailors are killed.

2001

September 11: Nineteen men hijack four U.S. passenger airplanes; two of the planes crash into the World Trade Center in New York City, one plane crashes into the Pentagon, and one crashes into a field in rural Pennsylvania; more than three thousand people die on the ground and in the airplanes.

October 7: U.S. and British forces begin bombing in Afghanistan, where the Taliban government has been sheltering Osama bin Laden and the al-Qaeda terrorist organization.

November 13: Kabul, the capital of Afghanistan, is abandoned by the Taliban, which swiftly disintegrates as the country's ruling government.

December 22: Richard Reid, a British citizen, attempts to detonate a bomb in his shoe while aboard an American Airlines flight from Paris to Miami. Reid fails to explode the bomb and is taken into custody.

2002

January 12: The first suspected terrorists arrive as detainees at a U.S. military base in Guantánamo, Cuba.

January 16: U.S. troops arrive in the Philippines to conduct joint training exercises with the Philippine army in the southern Philippines. U.S. advisers assist the Philippine troops in tracking members of Abu Sayyaf, a group designated as a terrorist organization by the United States.

January 29: President Bush describes Iran, Iraq, and North Korea as an "axis of evil," states that support and sponsor terrorism against the United States and the Western world.

March 2: Operation Anaconda, a U.S. offensive against al-Qaeda holdouts in the Shahi Kot valley of Afghanistan, begins. The offensive lasts until March 20 and ousts hundreds of al-Qaeda and Taliban fighters from the country.

May 1: U.S. troops arrive in Georgia, a former republic of the Soviet Union, to train local police in the investigation of terrorist groups.

June 8: In the Philippines an American and a Filipino, hostages of Abu Sayyaf, are killed during a rescue attempt.

July 16: The White House releases the Homeland Security Plan, drawn up to coordinate federal and local agencies in the prevention of terrorist attacks and in "first reaction" response to the use of conventional, chemical, biological, or nuclear weapons.

October 12: The Southeast Asian terrorist group Jemaah Islamiya bombs a popular nightclub on the island of Bali in Indonesia, killing more than two hundred people.

November 27: UN weapons inspectors return to Iraq. The government of Saddam Hussein has not cooperated with the United Nations inspection program since August 1998.

2003

January 27: UN inspectors report that Iraq is defying UN resolutions and demands to disarm.

March 1: Iraq begins destroying banned al-Samoud missiles in response to a second report that states it is still not cooperating with UN demands.

March 19: U.S. and British aircraft begin bombing runs over selected military targets in preparation for a ground offensive in Iraq, nicknamed Operation Iraqi Freedom.

April 10: U.S. military forces enter Baghdad, the capital of Iraq, in strength.

May 12: Suicide bombers attack three housing sites in the capital city of Riyadh, Saudi Arabia.

May 16: Twelve suicide bombers detonate cars at five different sites in Casablanca, Morocco, killing thirty-one people.

August 7: A car bomb explodes outside the Jordanian embassy in Baghdad, Iraq, killing nineteen people.

August 19: A car bomb explodes outside the UN headquarters in Baghdad, killing at least seventy-five people as well as the leader of the UN mission, Sergio Vieira de Mello.

August 29: Terrorists attack a Shiite mosque and holy site in the Iraqi city of Najaf, killing Ayatollah Mohammed Baqr al-Hakim, a Shiite cleric who had encouraged the Shiite community to cooperate with U.S. forces.

★ For Further Reading ★

Anonymous, *Through Our Enemies Eyes: Osama bin Laden, Radical Islam & the Future of America.* Washington, DC: Brasseys, 2003. The author, who is described as "an anonymous member of the U.S. intelligence community," explores radical Islam, the motivations of bin Laden and the members of al-Qaeda, and their ultimate goal in the destruction of Western influence in the Middle East and throughout the Muslim world.

Bruce Berkowitz, *The New Face of War: How War Will Be Fought in the 21st Century.* New York: Free Press, 2003. A look at new technologies and techniques of warfare, put to use by the United States in Afghanistan, Iraq, and against terrorist cells and leaders in the Middle East and South Asia. The author, a consultant to the Defense Department, describes the new war as a battle of decision making, in which troop strength counts less than fluid organization and the ability to process and react to information more quickly than the enemy.

John Collins and Ross Glover, eds., *Collateral Language: A User's Guide to America's New War.* New York: New York University Press, 2002. A series of essays on the terminology used by government and media sources in the War on Terrorism. The book gives insight to those studying the conflict and dealing with flexible terms such as "terrorism" and "radical fundamentalism," which are often employed as tools of persuasion.

Jane Corbin, *Al-Qaeda: In Search of the Terror Network That Threatens the World.* New York: Thunder's Mouth, 2002. A BBC journalist's account of al-Qaeda's attacks against U.S. installations in the 1990s, the September 11 attacks, and the run-up to the war against al-Qaeda in Afghanistan. The author goes into detail on the lives and thoughts of Osama bin Laden and many of the September 11 hijackers.

Jean Bethke Elshtain, *Just War Against Terror: The Burden of American Power in a Violent World.* New York: Basic Books, 2003. The author argues the ethical case for war and the use of violence against terrorists, claiming that the United States has a duty to suppress Islamic fundamentalists when they threaten universal human rights and aspirations.

Norman Friedman, *Terrorism, Afghanistan, and America's New Way of War.* Annapolis, MD: United States Naval Institute, 2003. The author analyzes the war in Afghanistan and the larger, ongoing War on Terrorism, asserting that the struggle has brought into being a new tactical and strategic approach by the armed forces.

Victor Davis Hanson, *An Autumn of War: What America Learned from September 11 and the War on Terrorism.* New York: Anchor, 2002. A collection of essays written in the aftermath of the September 11 attacks, in which the author describes the coming War on Terrorism, using a wide knowledge of military history to give the conflict perspective.

Eric L. Harney, *Inside Delta Force: The Story of America's Elite Counterterrorist Unit.* New York: Delacorte Press, 2002. A founder of the U.S. Army's Delta Force unit gives an insider's look at the formation of this unit, the training its members go through, missions it has carried out in the Middle East and elsewhere, and its future use as part of the "asymmetric warfare" tactics in the War on Terrorism.

Brian Michael Jenkins and Christopher Pike, *Countering Al Qaeda: An Appreciation of the Situation and Suggestions for Strategy.* Santa Monica, CA: Rand, 2002. The book analyzes the current condition of al-Qaeda and makes policy and military recommendations on the future war on terror.

Raoul Mahajan, *Full Spectrum Dominance: U.S. Power in Iraq and Beyond.* New York: Seven Stories, 2003. The author analyzes the rationale for the attack on Iraq in the spring of 2003 and asserts that the real motivation of the War on Terrorism is dominance, political and military, of the Middle East.

★ Works Consulted ★

Books

Robert Baer and Seymour M. Hersh, *See No Evil: The True Story of a Ground Soldier in the CIA's War on Terrorisrm.* New York: Three Rivers, 2002. An experienced field officer of the CIA recounts that organization's methods and mistakes, in the Middle East and elsewhere, and how a culture of "political correctness" within the agency hamstrung the efforts of its operatives.

Peter L. Bergen, *Holy War, Inc.: Inside the Secret World of Osama bin Laden.* New York: Free Press, 2001. Published just after the September 11 attacks, this book reviews Osama bin Laden's career in Sudan and Afghanistan and details the organization of al-Qaeda and how it carried out the September 11 attacks.

Kurt M. Campbell and Michele A. Flournoy, *To Prevail: An American Strategy for the Campaign Against Terrorism.* Washington, DC: Center for Strategic and International Studies, 2001. A Washington think tank's detailed strategy for the future war against terrorism, with recommendations for military and diplomatic action and a breakdown, country by country, of proper American policy and objectives relating to terrorism.

Bill Gertz, *Breakdown: The Failure of American Intelligence to Defeat Global Terror.* New York: Penguin, 2002. The author describes the shortcomings of the CIA and FBI and how complacency, bureaucratic rivalries, and political agendas prevented these agencies from detecting and preventing terrorist attacks carried out by al-Qaeda and others.

Dore Gold, *Hatred's Kingdom: How Saudi Arabia Supports the New Global Terrorism.* Washington, DC: Regnery, 2003. The author describes Saudi Arabia's regime and society, designating that country and its brand of Wahhabi Islam as the true source of modern terrorist movements.

Rohan Gunaratna, *Inside Al Qaeda: Global Network of Terror.* New York: Berkeley, 2002. The author presents in great detail, some of it based on slim evidence, the activities of al-Qaeda and Osama bin Laden during the 1990s.

Katrina Vanden Heuvel and Jonathan Schell, eds., *A Just Response:* The Nation *on Terrorism, Democracy, and September 11, 2001.* New York: Thunder's Mouth, 2002. Essays published in the *Nation* in the aftermath of September 11, in which the authors debate the proper response to the attacks and the best ways of suppressing terrorism around the globe.

Bruce Hoffman, *Inside Terrorism.* New York: Columbia University Press, 1999. The author offers a broad introduction to the history of terrorism in the twentieth century.

John Pynchon Holmes, *Terrorism: Today's Biggest Threat to Freedom.* New York: Pinnacle, 2001. A book originally published in 1994 and updated immediately after the September 2001 attacks. Includes brief but useful sketches of the major terrorist organizations, grouped in alphabetical order, and a very general overview of terrorist methods and counterterrorism measures.

Roland Jacquard, *In the Name of Osama Bin Laden: Global Terrorism and the Bin Laden Brotherhood.* Durham, NC: Duke University Press, 2002. This analysis of al-Qaeda by a French author was published in September 2001, and became an immediate international best seller. The author offers interesting detail on bin Laden's years in Sudan and Afghanistan.

Anthony Lake, *Six Nightmares: Real Threats in a Dangerous World and How America Can Meet Them.* Boston: Little, Brown, 2000. The author was a national security adviser to President Clinton. Using fictional scenarios, he details worst-case terrorist actions that might be taken against the United States. Lake also describes how the ongoing political rivalries and contests in Washington distort and undermine military preparedness, intelligence activities, and foreign policy decisions.

Michael A. Ledeen, *The War Against the Terror Masters: Why It Happened. Where We Are Now. How We'll Win,* New York: St. Martin's, 2002. An eloquent and opinionated overview of the War on Terrorism, in which the author blames the government's complacency during the 1990s for the rise of al-Qaeda and other groups, and calls for a direct confrontation with nations that harbor or support terrorism, including Syria, Iraq, and Iran.

Bill Sammon, *Fighting Back: The War on Terrorism—from Inside the Bush White House.* Washington, DC: Regnery, 2002. A detailed, and very uncritical, account of the actions of President Bush on September 11 and in the months following. The author focuses on Bush's interaction with his staff and ordinary citizens, and on the strategic decisions taken in the weeks following the attack.

Bob Woodward, *Bush at War.* New York: Simon and Schuster, 2002. The author gives a day-by-day and blow-by-blow account of the Afghanistan war from inside the White House. This book is most valuable for the insights it provides into planning and decision making by the White House staff, the National Security Council, and the Defense Department.

Periodicals

Robert Baer, "The Fall of the House of Saud," *Atlantic Monthly,* May 2003.

Walden Bello, "A 'Second Front' in the Philippines," *Nation,* March 18, 2002.

Stephen Biddle, "Afghanistan and the Future of Warfare," *Foreign Affairs,* March/April 2003.

Wesley Clark, "An Army of One?" *Washington Monthly,* September 2002.

Miral Fahmy, "Bin Laden Aide Urges Muslims to Strike U.S., Jews," *Reuters News Service,* May 21, 2003.

Jeff Jacoby, "A Growing Rift with Europe," *Boston Globe,* June 5, 2003.

David E. Kaplan, "Taking Offense: The Inside Story of How U.S. Terrorist Hunters Are Going After al Qaeda," *U.S. News & World Report,* June 2, 2003.

Anatol Lieven, "The Pressures on Pakistan," *Foreign Affairs,* January/February 2001.

Johanna McGeary, "Next Stop Mindanao," *Time,* January 28, 2002.

Ahmed Rashid and Barnett Rubin, "S.O.S. from Afghanistan," *Wall Street Journal,* May 29, 2003.

Eric Rouleau, "Trouble in the Kingdom," *Foreign Affairs,* July/August 2002.

Jonathan Stevenson, "How Europe and America Defend Themselves" *Foreign Affairs,* March/April 2003.

Fareed Zakaria, "Now Saudis See the Enemy," *Newsweek,* May 26, 2003.

Internet Sources

About the Philippines, "The 1987 Constitution of the Republic of the Philippines: Article XVIII," August 20, 2003. www.gov.ph.

Amit Baruah, "An Exercise in Intervention," *Frontline,* August 20, 2003. www.frontlineonnet.com

Philip Bowring, "Manila Can't Depend upon an American Crutch," *International Herald Tribune,* May 19, 2003. www.iht.com.

CNN.com, "Qaddafi: 'Libya Is Against Terrorism,'" July 11, 2002. www.cnn.com.

———, "Transcript of President Bush's Address," September 21, 2001. www.cnn.com.

Fred Kaplan, "The Flaw in Shock and Awe," Slate.com, March 26, 2003. http://slate.msn.com.

Lara Logan, "On the Scene: The Fall of Baghdad," CBSNews.com, April 9, 2003. www.cbsnews.com.

Jamie McIntyre, "U.S. Propaganda to Taliban: 'You Are Condemned,'" CNN.com, October 18, 2001. www.cnn.com.

Office of the Coordinator for Counterterrorism, "Overview of State-Sponsored Terrorism," U.S. Department of State, April 2001. www.state.gov.

———, "Patterns of Global Terrorism," U.S. Department of State, August 20, 2003. www.state.gov.

James S. Robbins, "Freedom Eagle: The Mission in the Philippines," *National Review,* January 18, 2002. www.nationalreview.com.

U.S. Department of Justice, "Al Qaeda Training Manual." www.usdoj.gov.

Imran Waheed, "Egypt/Uzbekistan Crooked Partners in the 'War on Terrorism,'" Khilafah.com. www.khilafah.com.

Websites

CBSNews.com (www.cbsnews.com). A collection of reports, video, audio, graphics, and background information from the national television network's news department.

CNN.com (www.cnn.com). Useful website of the global CNN network, giving background information on current terrorism issues and a compehensive back file of documents, speeches, and reports related to important terrorist events.

Frontlineonnet.com (www.frontlineonnet.com). The website of India's national magazine, associated with the *Hindu* newspaper, including articles covering events in India as well as Southeast Asia.

The *International Herald Tribune* Online (www.iht.com). The website of the *International Herald Tribune,* an English-language daily published in Paris and carrying articles from the *New York Times* and the *Washington Post.*

North Atlantic Treaty Organization (www.nato.int). NATO's official website publishes an online collection of treaties, speeches, and other important documents.

✯ Index ✯

☆ Picture Credits ☆

Cover: © AFP/CORBIS
AP Wide World Photos, 15, 25, 27, 28, 41, 49, 51, 62-63, 76, 80, 88
Department of Defense photo by R.D. Ward, 44
Department of Defense photo by Helene C. Stikkel, 68
Jeff Christensen/Reuters/Landov, 12
Nick Didlick/Reuters/Landov, 32
Maurizio Gambarini/Landov, 54
Markus Hansen/DPA/Landov, 85
Chris Jouan, 30
Mian Khursheed/Reuters/Landov, 72
Reuters/Landov, 20, 48, 59, 64, 77, 82, 92
U.S. Air Force photo by Staff Sgt. Steven Pearsall, 17
U.S. Navy photo by Photographer's Mate First Class Tim Turner, 23

✫ About the Author ✫

Tom Streissguth was born in Washington, D.C., and raised in Minneapolis. He has worked as a teacher, editor, and journalist, and has traveled widely in Europe, the Middle East, and Southeast Asia. He has written more than fifty works of nonfiction—histories, biographies, and geography books—for young readers. He currently lives in southern Florida.